PICTURE
ENCYCLOPEDIA

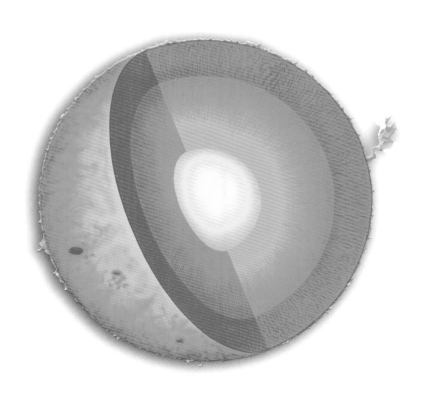

PICTURE ENCYCLOPEDIA

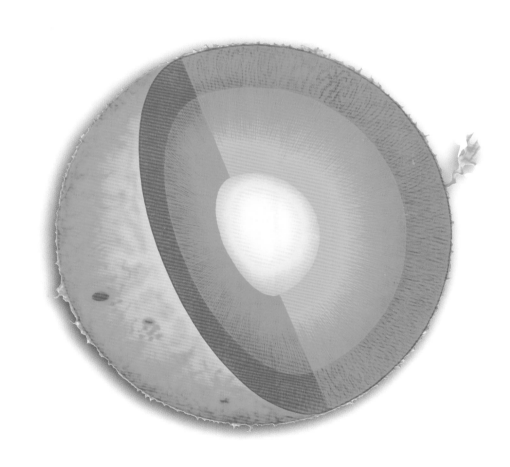

Author and Editor
Neil Morris

This is a Parragon Publishing Book
This edition published in 2004

Parragon Publishing
Queen Street House
4 Queen Street
Bath BA1 1HE, UK

British Library Cataloguing-in-Publication Data

A catalogue record for this book is available from the British Library.

ISBN 1-40540-520-1

Printed in Indonesia

Contents

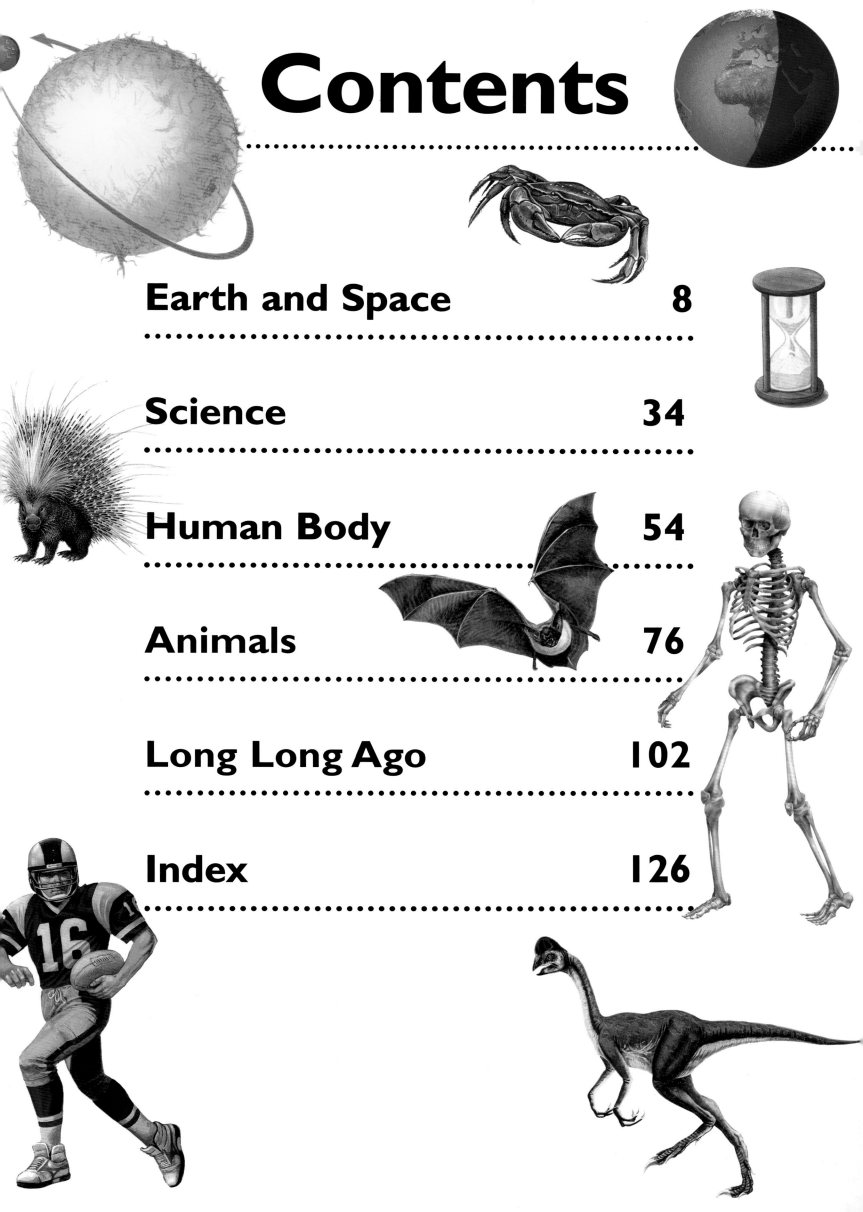

Introduction

An encyclopedia is a book that contains all kinds of information. In this children's encyclopedia, the information is presented in five sections: Earth and Space, Science, Human Body, Animals, and Long Long Ago. Each of these sections gives a wide coverage of the subject matter, offering information through different topics.

All the information in this book is presented in an interesting, highly visual way. There are hundreds of photographs, illustrations, and even cartoons, all with explanatory text. Extra captions offer fascinating facts. Of course, no encyclopedia of this size can possibly cover every topic, but the comprehensive index is there to help readers find the information they are looking for.

To add to the interest, each section has many simple projects. In each case, the clear photograph shows the end result that is possible and acts as an encouragement to attempt the project. Some are fun craft ideas, while others are easy experiments.

Above all, this book is meant to interest, entertain, and amuse children. It is intended to be fun to use and dip into, so that children will come back to it... again and again.

Our Planet

We live on the planet Earth. On our planet there are high mountains and hot deserts, huge oceans and freezing cold regions. A blanket of air is wrapped around the Earth. This air allows us to breathe and live. Beyond the air, our planet is surrounded by space. A long way away in space, there are other planets and stars. Most planets have satellites, or moons, which circle around them.

△ **From space, Earth** looks like a mainly blue and white planet. It looks blue because water covers most of its surface. The white swirling patterns are clouds, and the brown and green areas are land.

Earth has a diameter of about 7,900 miles (12,700 km), almost four times bigger than the Moon. The Moon is about 240,000 miles (385,000 km) away from Earth.

The Moon circles the Earth once a month. On its journey, different amounts of its sunlit side can be seen from Earth. This makes the Moon seem to change shape during the month.

△ **The Moon spins** as it circles the Earth, so the same side always faces us. People had never seen the other side of the Moon until a spacecraft traveled around it.

△ **The Moon** was probably formed when a huge asteroid crashed into the Earth billions of years ago. The crash threw rock fragments into space, and these came together to form the Moon.

▷ **The Moon's surface** is full of craters. These were formed by chunks of space rock crashing into it. There is no air or water on the Moon, so it is odd that we call the Moon's vast, dry plains "seas."

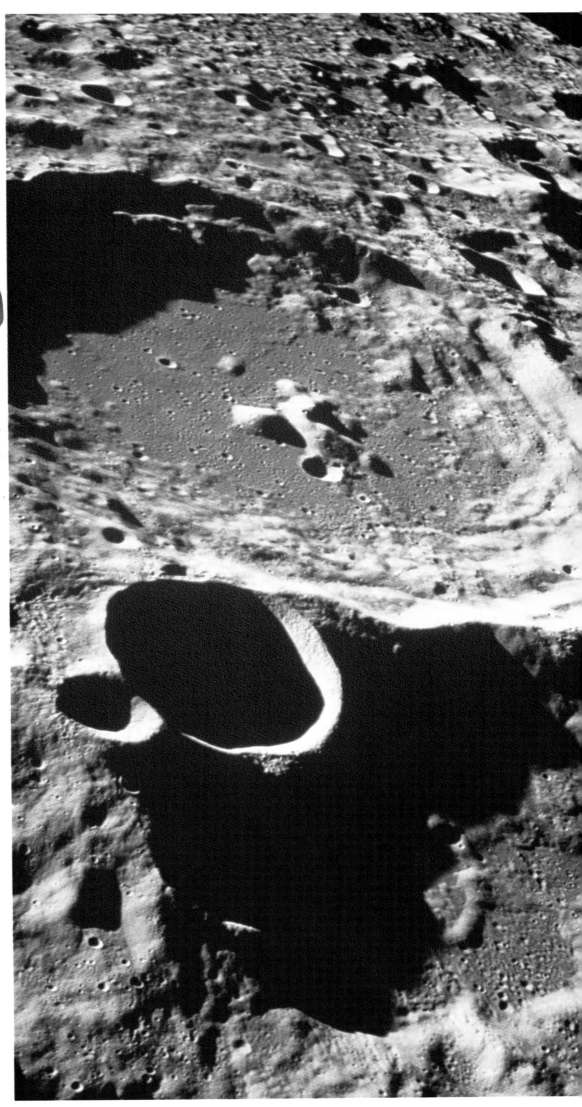

The Solar System

Nine planets, including Earth, travel around the Sun. Along with moons, comets, and lumps of rock, they make up the Solar System.

This system is Earth's local neighborhood in space. Everything in it is connected to the Sun by a force that we cannot see. This force is called gravity.

The largest planet, Jupiter, is big enough to hold over 1,300 Earths. The smallest planet, Pluto, is smaller even than our Moon.

▽ **Among the planets** there are four giants— Jupiter, Saturn, Uranus, and Neptune. Each has a small rocky core, surrounded by a thick layer of ice or liquid, with gas on the outside. Along with Pluto, these giants are called the outer planets.

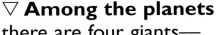

Mercury

Venus

Earth

Mars

Jupiter

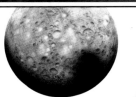

PLASTICINE PLANETS
Mold Plasticine around beads, marbles and ping-pong balls to make planets. Earth can be blue and white, Mars red, and Jupiter orange. Mold a big yellow Sun around a tennis ball. Use black cardboard for a space background and arrange the nine planets in the right order. You could put a label next to each one.

Pluto

Neptune

Uranus

Saturn

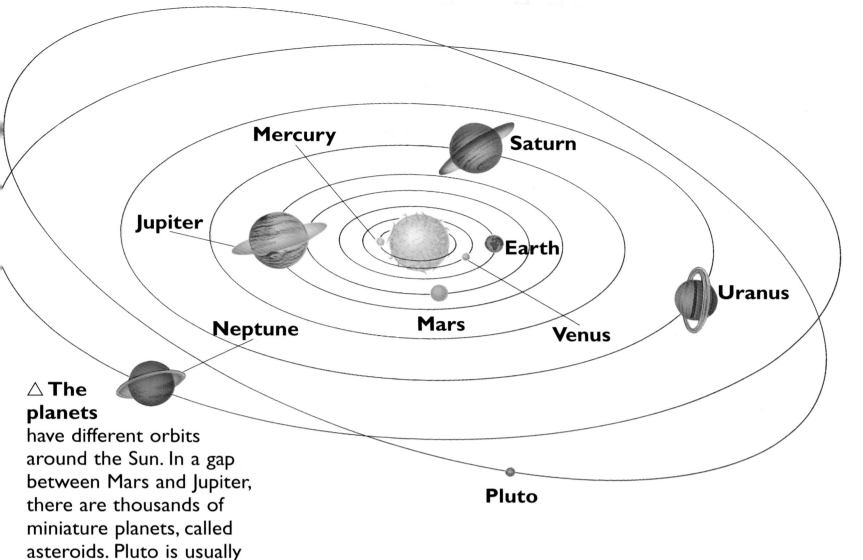

Mercury

Jupiter

Saturn

Earth

Neptune

Mars

Venus

Uranus

Pluto

△ **The planets** have different orbits around the Sun. In a gap between Mars and Jupiter, there are thousands of miniature planets, called asteroids. Pluto is usually the farthest planet from the Sun, but sometimes its path crosses Neptune's.

Mercury is a small, rocky planet. It is closest to the Sun and travels around it six times in one of our Earth years.

NEW WORDS

comet A snowball of ice and dust that travels around the Sun.

gravity A force that pulls everything toward it.

orbit To travel around something.

solar To do with the Sun.

PLANETS NAMED AFTER GODS

Mercury, messenger of the gods

Venus, goddess of love

Mars, god of war

Jupiter, king of the gods

Saturn, father of Jupiter

Uranus, god of the heavens

Neptune, god of the sea

Pluto, god of the underworld

Our Star

Aquarius,
the Water-carrier,
Jan 20-Feb 18

Pisces,
the Fish,
Feb 19-Mar 20

Aries,
the Ram,
Mar 21-Apr 19

Taurus,
the Bull,
Apr 20-May

Our Solar System has one star, which we call the Sun. Stars burn, and the sunlight that gives us life is the light of our burning star.

The Sun is a vast, fiery ball of gases. The hottest part of the Sun is its core, where energy is produced. The Sun burns steadily and its energy provides the Earth with heat and light. We could not live without the Sun's light, which takes just over eight minutes to travel through space and reach us.

You must never look directly at the Sun. Its light is so strong that this would harm your eyes.

photosphere

sunspot

Twinkle, twinkle, little star
Seen from Earth, stars seem to twinkle. This is because starlight passes through bands of hot and cold air around the Earth, and this makes the light flicker. In space, stars shine steadily.

▷ **Heat from the core** surges up to the Sun's surface, called the photosphere. Sunspots are dark, cooler patches. Prominences are jets of gas that erupt from the surface.

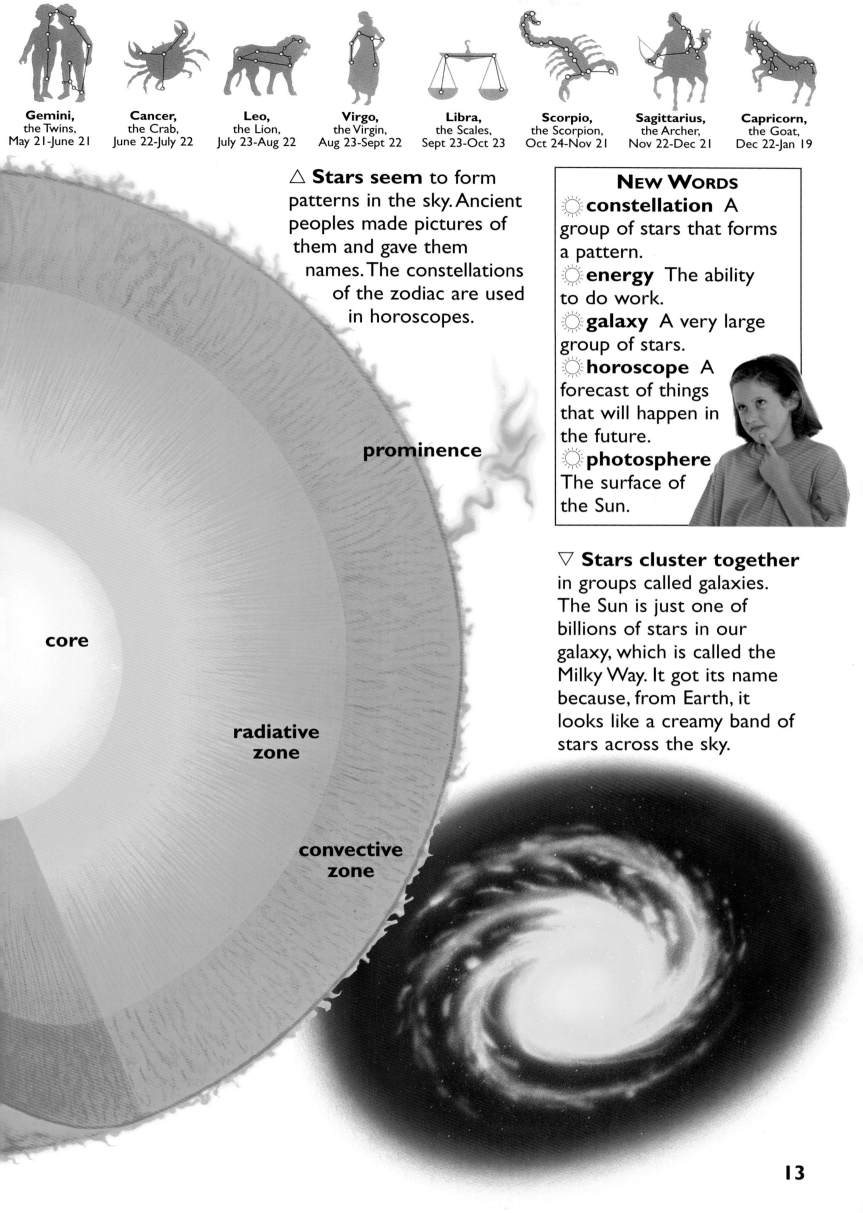

Gemini,
the Twins,
May 21-June 21

Cancer,
the Crab,
June 22-July 22

Leo,
the Lion,
July 23-Aug 22

Virgo,
the Virgin,
Aug 23-Sept 22

Libra,
the Scales,
Sept 23-Oct 23

Scorpio,
the Scorpion,
Oct 24-Nov 21

Sagittarius,
the Archer,
Nov 22-Dec 21

Capricorn,
the Goat,
Dec 22-Jan 19

△ **Stars seem** to form patterns in the sky. Ancient peoples made pictures of them and gave them names. The constellations of the zodiac are used in horoscopes.

prominence

core

radiative zone

convective zone

NEW WORDS

☼ **constellation** A group of stars that forms a pattern.
☼ **energy** The ability to do work.
☼ **galaxy** A very large group of stars.
☼ **horoscope** A forecast of things that will happen in the future.
☼ **photosphere** The surface of the Sun.

▽ **Stars cluster together** in groups called galaxies. The Sun is just one of billions of stars in our galaxy, which is called the Milky Way. It got its name because, from Earth, it looks like a creamy band of stars across the sky.

13

▷ **Scientists believe that** millions of years after the Big Bang, gases clustered into clouds. These clouds clumped together to form galaxies.

The planets formed later from clouds of gas, dust, and rocks. As the Universe expands, the galaxies are moving farther apart.

galaxies form

△ **There are countless** billions of stars in the Universe. Sometimes a very old star explodes. We call this a supernova. New stars are being created all the time in different sizes.

▽ **The Sun** is an ordinary yellow star. It is much bigger than a red dwarf star, which is half as hot. A blue giant is at least four times hotter than the Sun. A red supergiant is five hundred times the Sun's width.

NEW WORDS
🌀 **expand** To become larger.
🌀 **scientist** A person who studies the way things work.
🌀 **supernova** A very old star when it explodes.

red dwarf

yellow star (like the Sun)

blue giant

red supergian

14

The Universe

Our address in space is "Earth, Solar System, Milky Way Galaxy, Universe." The Universe is the biggest thing there is and includes all the empty parts of space between the stars.

Most scientists think that the Universe began with a Big Bang, which happened billions of years ago. Since then it has been growing bigger and bigger in all directions, creating more and more space.

the Big Bang

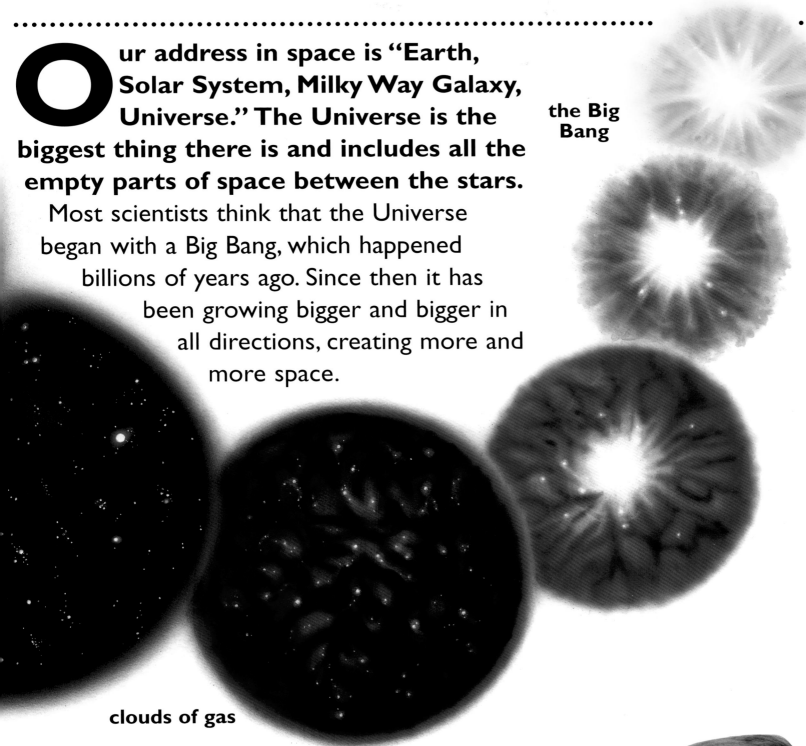

clouds of gas

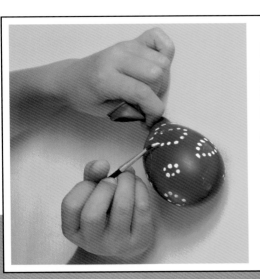

UNIVERSAL BALLOON

Paint white, squiggly, galaxy shapes on a large blue balloon. Let the paint dry, and then slowly blow up the balloon. You will see the galaxies moving apart on the balloon, just as they are doing in the Universe.

Days and Seasons

As the Earth travels around the Sun, it spins like a top. It turns right around once every 24 hours, and this gives us day and night.

The part of the Earth facing the Sun is in daylight. When that part turns away from the Sun, it gets dark and has nighttime.

We have seasons because the Earth has a tilt, so that north and south are not straight up and down. When the northern half of the Earth is tilted toward the Sun, it is summer there. At that time it is winter in the southern half of the world, because it is tilted away from the Sun's warmth.

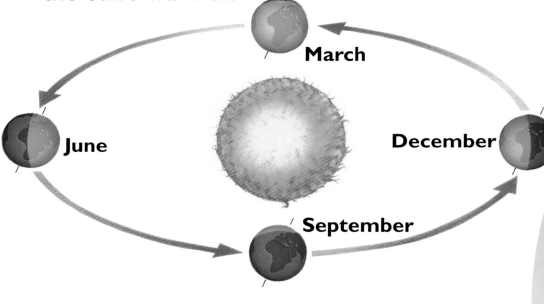

March

December

June

September

spring

△ **In June** the northern part of the Earth is tilted toward the Sun. It is summer there then, with long, light days and short, dark nights. In December it is the exact opposite. Then the Sun shines more directly on the southern part and makes it warmer.

🌳 **It takes a year** for the Earth to travel all the way around the Sun. During that time the Earth spins round 365 times, giving that number of days. At the same time the Moon travels around the Earth 12 times, giving that number of months.

16

NIGHT AND DAY

In a darkened room, shine a flashlight at a globe of the Earth. If you don't have a globe, use a large ball. The globe or ball is the Earth, and your flashlight acts like the Sun as it shines on our planet. The side facing the Sun gets light, so there it is day. On the dark side of the globe it is night. You could slowly spin the Earth around, to see how day and night follow each other around the globe.

In some places around the middle of the Earth, near the equator, there are only two seasons. One part of the year is hot and dry, and the other part is warm and wet.

▽ **The Earth's landscape** changes with the seasons. Many trees grow new leaves in spring. The leaves are green and fully grown in summer. They turn brown and start to fall in autumn. In winter, the trees' branches are bare.

winter

summer

autumn

Traveling in Space

Spacecraft are blasted into space by powerful rockets. Once the rocket has used up its fuel, the spacecraft carries on under its own power.

Astronauts are space travelers. They live and work in space, sometimes for months on end. Astronauts have to do special training, because there is so little gravity in space. This means that everything in a spacecraft floats, including the astronauts.

▷ **A space shuttle** is a reusable spacecraft. It rides on a huge fuel tank to take off, uses its own power in space, and lands back on Earth like a plane. Shuttles are used to take astronauts to a space station.

◁ **In 1969,** American astronauts visited the Moon for the first time. They landed in a lunar module and wore spacesuits to walk on the Moon's surface. The suits protected them, provided them with air to breathe and kept them at the right temperature.

The first living thing to travel in space was a dog named Laika, in 1957. On April 12, 1961, Russian Yuri Gagarin circled the Earth once to become the first person in space. Just a few weeks later, Alan Shepard became the first U.S. astronaut. His space flight lasted just about 15 minutes.

▷ **Astronauts can travel** a short distance away from their spacecraft by putting a special jet-unit on their back. They can move or turn in any direction with this Manned Maneuvering Unit attached to them.

NEW WORDS

astronaut A person who travels in space.

lunar module The part of a spaceship that lands on the Moon.

magnetic Able to stick to metal objects by the power of magnetism.

space station A spaceship in which astronauts can live and work.

What do astronauts eat?
Most space food is dried, to save weight. Water is added to the food packets before they are heated. Astronauts have to hold on to their food, otherwise it just floats around the spacecraft. All knives and forks are magnetic, so that they stick to the meal trays.

PLANET EARTH PUZZLE

Place a piece of tracing paper on the map at the bottom of this page. Trace the thick lines of the plates with a black felt pen, and add the outlines of the continents in pencil. Stick the traced map onto cardboard and color it in. Cut the map up into separate pieces to make your jigsaw puzzle. Jumble up the pieces, then use the plate lines to help you fit your puzzle together again.

The Earth's crust is cracked into huge pieces that fit together like a giant jigsaw puzzle. These pieces are called plates. The Earth's oceans and continents are split up by the plates, which float on the mantle.

NEW WORDS

continent A huge land mass.

core The central part of the Earth.

crust The Earth's outer shell.

mantle A thick layer of hot rock.

molten Melted, or turned into hot liquid.

plate A piece of the Earth's crust.

▽ **Earth** looks cool from space, because of its water. Inside, the center is hot. It is nearly 4,000 miles (6,000 km) from Earth's surface.

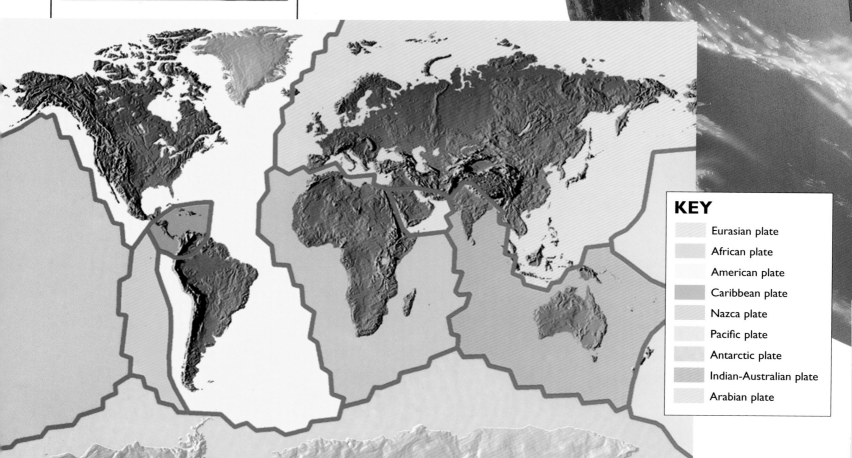

KEY

	Eurasian plate
	African plate
	American plate
	Caribbean plate
	Nazca plate
	Pacific plate
	Antarctic plate
	Indian-Australian plate
	Arabian plate

Inside the Earth

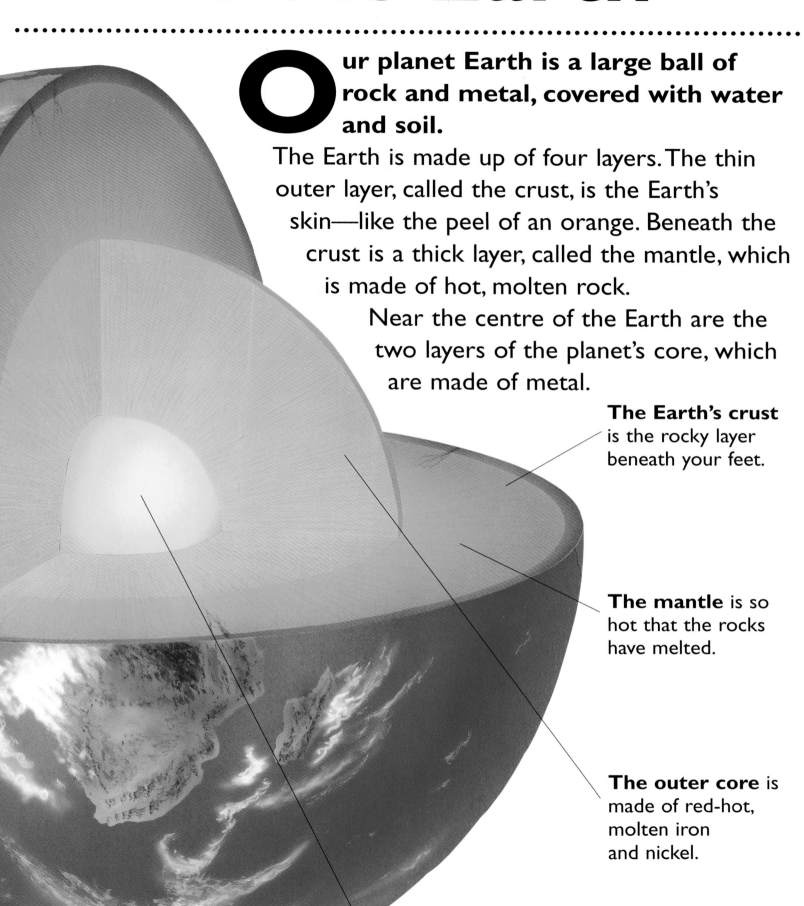

Our planet Earth is a large ball of rock and metal, covered with water and soil.

The Earth is made up of four layers. The thin outer layer, called the crust, is the Earth's skin—like the peel of an orange. Beneath the crust is a thick layer, called the mantle, which is made of hot, molten rock.

Near the centre of the Earth are the two layers of the planet's core, which are made of metal.

The Earth's crust is the rocky layer beneath your feet.

The mantle is so hot that the rocks have melted.

The outer core is made of red-hot, molten iron and nickel.

The inner core is an iron ball. Although it is solid, this is the hottest part of the planet.

21

Volcanoes and Earthquakes

△ **The San Andreas Fault**, in California, shows where two of the Earth's plates slide past each other. They move about 2 inches (5 cm) a year.

The plates that make up the Earth's crust slowly move and rub against each other. Though they only move a few inches each year, their buckling can cause volcanoes and earthquakes.

Volcanoes and earthquakes usually form near the edge of plates. Many of them happen in a region around the Pacific Ocean called the "Ring of Fire." They sometimes cause giant waves called tsunamis.

The strongest recorded earthquake happened in Ecuador in 1906. It measured 8.6 on the Richter scale, which is used to measure the strength of earthquakes. In 1995, an earthquake at Kobe, in Japan, killed 5,500 people and damaged 190,000 buildings.

◁ **Overpasses and bridges** are at great risk when they are shaken by an earthquake. The quake's waves move out from a point called the epicenter. Very often there are minor tremors before and after a big earthquake.

The world's largest active volcano is Mauna Loa, in Hawaii. It rises to 13,680 feet (4,170 m) above sea level, and is over 30,000 feet (9,000 m) high when measured from the ocean bed. It usually erupts about once every four years.

A volcano that has not erupted for a long time is called dormant, or "sleeping." If a volcano has done nothing at all for thousands of years, it is said to be extinct.

▽ **When a volcano** erupts, red-hot lava blasts up through an opening in the Earth's crust. The steep sides of a volcano mountain are made of layers of hardened lava and ash. These layers build up with each eruption.

NEW WORDS
epicenter The center of an earthquake, where the waves of shaking earth come from.
lava Melted rock that flows from a volcano.
tremor A shaking movement.
tsunami A giant wave that can cause great damage.

Water

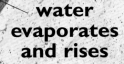

water droplets fall

water vapor forms clouds

water evaporates and rises

Water falls from clouds in the sky in the form of rain, snow, or hail.

When rainwater falls on the land, some of it seeps into the ground and is held in rocks below the surface. In limestone areas, this water makes underground caves. Some water collects in lakes, but most forms rivers that finally find their way to the sea.

△ **Water goes round** in a never-ending cycle. First, it evaporates from the oceans. The water vapor rises and turns into clouds. When the droplets in the clouds get too heavy, they fall to land as rain. Some rain flows back to the oceans, and then the water cycle starts all over again.

MEASURING RAIN

To make your own rain gauge, use an empty jar. Pour in a cup of water, I tbsp (200 ml) at a time. Use a marker pen to mark tbsp.(10 ml) levels on the jar. Empty the jar and put in a funnel. Then put your gauge outside to catch the rain.

NEW WORDS

cave An underground tunnel.

evaporate To turn into a vapor or gas.

gauge An instrument that measures something.

limestone A soft kind of rock.

mineral A hard substance that is usually found in the ground in rock form.

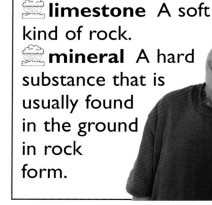

In caves, minerals in dripping water make stalactites. These hang down from the roof of the cave, while stalagmites grow up from the ground. Sometimes they meet up to form a column.

◁ **Most underground caves** are made by running water. Over many years, rainwater wears away at cracks in soft limestone rocks. The cracks grow wider, making holes and then wide passages. Constantly dripping water creates fantastic rock shapes inside caves.

▷ **Where a river** drops over the edge of a hard rockface, it becomes a waterfall. Victoria Falls plunges 420 feet (130 m) on the Zambezi River in Africa.

▽ **This cross-section** shows how water wears away limestone rocks and hollows out caves. The stream on the surface drops into a sinkhole and forms a shaft.

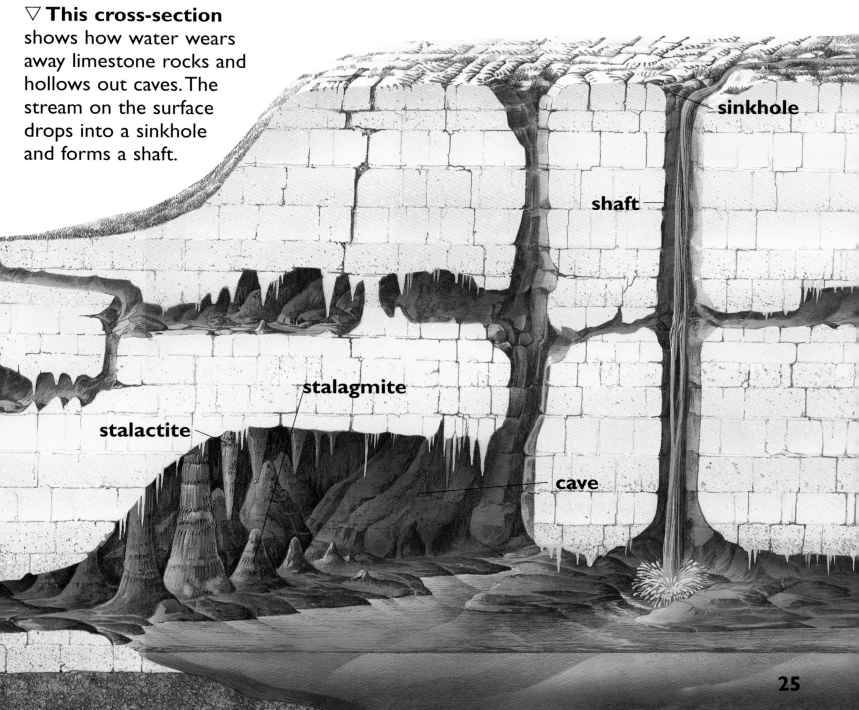

sinkhole

shaft

stalagmite

stalactite

cave

Mountains

There are high mountains all over the world. They took millions of years to form, as the plates that make up the Earth's crust squeezed and buckled.

Mountain ranges that lie near the edge of plates are still being pushed higher. They have steep, rocky peaks. Older ranges that lie further from the plate edges have been worn away over the years by rain, wind, and ice.

It is cold on high mountains, and the peaks have no plants.

NEW WORDS

⛰ **crag** A steep piece of rough rock.

⛰ **range** A group or series of mountains.

⛰ **strata** Layers of rock.

△ **The Earth's plates** are made up of layers of rock, called strata. As the plates move, the strata are bent into folds. In the mountains, you can often see how the layers have been folded into wavy lines.

▷ **The longest** mountain range on land is the Andes, which stretches for over 4,000 miles (7,000 km) down the west coast of South America. The Transantarctic Mountains stretch right across the frozen continent of Antarctica.

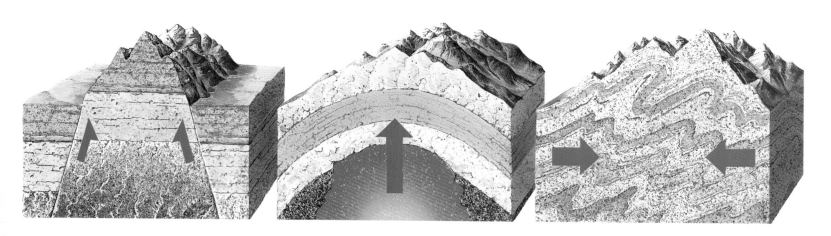

△ **Block mountains** are created when the Earth's crust develops cracks, called faults, and the chunk of land between them is pushed up.

△ **Dome mountains** form when the top layers of the Earth's crust are pushed up by molten rock underneath. This makes a big bulge.

△ **Fold mountains** are formed when one plate bumps and pushes against another. Rock is squeezed up into folds. The Andes were made this way.

Mountains are often joined together in a series, or range. The longest and highest ranges, such as the Andes and the Himalayas, form huge mountain systems. Few animals or people live on the highest mountains.

MOUNTAINS OF JUNK
Crumple newspaper into big balls and tape them onto a cardboard base. Make papier-mâché pulp by soaking newspaper pieces in a bucket of wallpaper paste. Cover the balls with the pulp to make mountains and valleys. When your landscape is dry, paint some snow-capped peaks with white paint. Sprinkle the base with sand. You could add a mountain lake.

What is an ibex?
The ibex is a wild mountain goat that lives in the high mountains in some parts of the world. Ibexes are sure-footed and happy to climb along rocky crags. Male ibexes have long horns, which they sometimes use to fight each other.

The ten highest mountains on land are all in the Himalayas, to the north of India. The highest peak of all, Mount Everest, lies on the border between Nepal and Tibet. It is 29,028 feet (8,848 m) high and is known to people of Tibet as Chomolongma, or "goddess mother of the world".

northern forest

temperate forest

▷ **The needle-leaved trees** of northern forests are called conifers. They bear their seeds in cones. Trees such as fir, pine, spruce, and larch have to survive long,

▽ **The massive sequoia trees** in California are evergreen conifers, and some are thousands of years old. The largest is nearly 300 feet (90 m) tall, with a diameter of 36 feet (11 m). Imagine trying to climb to the top!

▷ **Ash, beech, maple, and oak trees** all grow in temperate forests. In the autumn, their leaves turn brown. Then they shed their leaves to save water and help them get through the winter.

Forests

oak leaf

Almost a third of the Earth's land surface is covered with forests. The trees that grow in forests vary according to the region's climate—how warm it is, how long the winter lasts, and how much rain falls in that region.

Cool northern forests are full of evergreen trees. Temperate forests have deciduous trees that lose their leaves in winter. And tropical rain forests have an enormous variety of big, fast-growing trees.

NEW WORDS

climate The weather conditions of an area.

conifer A tree that makes its seeds in cones.

deciduous tree A tree that loses its leaves in the autumn.

evergreen tree A tree that keeps its leaves.

▽ **Rain forests** grow on warm, wet lowlands. Most rain forest trees are evergreen. It rains almost every day in a rain forest.

The taiga is the world's largest forest, stretching 6,000 miles (10,000 km) across northern Russia. The taiga is very cold during the long, dark winters, and summer in the forest is short and cool.

Millions of creatures live in rain forests, as there is plenty of warmth, water, and food. In the tropical rain forests there are parrots and toucans, monkeys and jaguars, frogs and snakes.

 The Amazon rain forest is the biggest in the world. Parts are being cut down at an alarming rate.

rain forest

Deserts

scorpion

New Words

cactus A fleshy, spiny plant that can store water.

dune A hill of sand.

oasis A place in the desert where there is water and plants can grow.

plain An area of flat country.

Most deserts are in hot parts of the world, where it is dry nearly all the time.

Some deserts are covered with huge, high sand dunes. But there are many other desert landscapes, including rocky hills and stony plains. In the world's largest desert, the Sahara in northern Africa, the temperature often reaches 120°F (49°C). Despite the heat and lack of water, these are not empty wastelands. Plants such as the cactus and animals such as the scorpion, and even some people, have become used to life in the desert.

Most deserts have small areas of water, where plants can grow and people can live. They are called oases. The Sahara has about 90 large oases.

▽ **In many desert regions**, rocks have been worn away over millions of years by the effects of heat and wind. The deserts of North America are full of strange-shaped, dramatic rock forms.

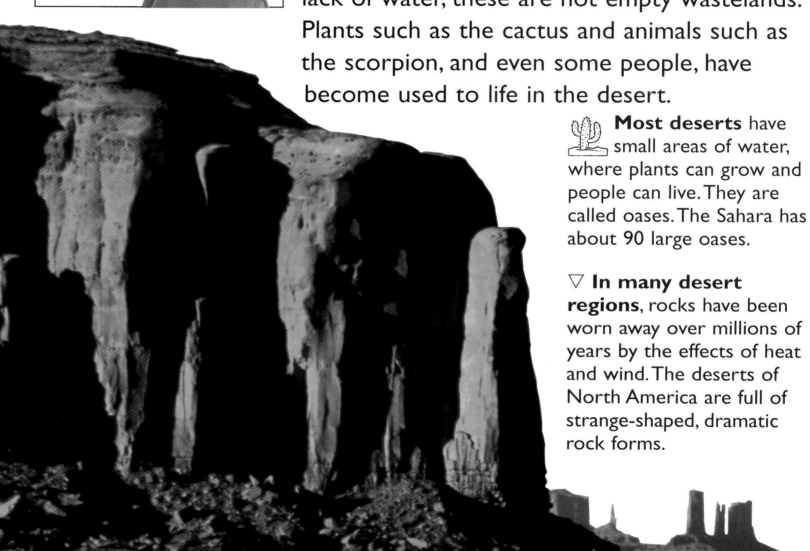

BAKING DESERT

Mix smooth dough from 6 cups of flour, 3 cups of salt, 6 tablespoons of cooking oil and water. Roll the dough and shape it into a desert landscape. Bake the desert at the bottom of the oven at a low temperature for 40 minutes. When it has cooled down, paint with glue and sprinkle with sand. Paint a green oasis, and add tissue-paper palm trees and, perhaps, a clay camel for effect.

△ **Some of the Sahara's** sand dunes are up to 1,500 feet (450 m) high. They are like seas of sand, and they change and drift with the action of the wind.

▷ **Cactus plants** store water in their fleshy stems. The giant saguaro cactus can grow over 55 feet (16 m) tall. Other desert plants suddenly shoot up if it rains, flower quickly and scatter their seeds.

Polar Regions

▽ **There are icebergs** in the cold sea near both Poles. They are huge chunks of floating freshwater ice that break off from glaciers and ice shelves. Only about a seventh of an iceberg appears above the water, so they are much bigger than they look.

Near the North and South Poles, at the very top and bottom of the world, it is very cold.

The region around the North Pole is called the Arctic. This is a huge area of frozen sea. The Arctic Ocean is covered in thick ice, which spreads over a wider area in winter. Some Arctic people, such as the Inuit and the Lapps, live on frozen land in the north of Asia, Europe, and North America.

The South Pole is on the frozen land of Antarctica, which is renowned as the coldest continent on Earth.

The largest iceberg ever seen was about 200 miles (300 km) long and 65 miles (100 km) wide. It was in the South Pacific Ocean.

◁ **Norwegian explorer Roald Amundsen** was first to reach the South Pole, in 1911. British explorer Robert Scott arrived a few weeks later, to find the Norwegian flag already flying there. At the South Pole, every way you look is north.

NEW WORDS

crevasse A deep crack in ice.

glacier A river of ice that moves very slowly.

iceberg A huge chunk of ice floating in the sea.

treaty A special, signed agreement between countries.

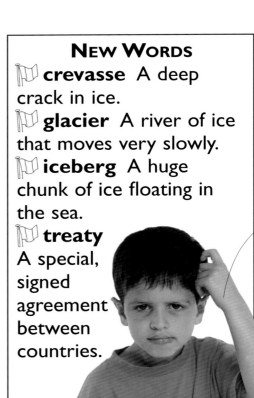

◁ **A glacier** is a mass of ice that moves slowly down a mountain like a river. As a glacier flows downhill, it often cracks into deep openings called crevasses.

In Antarctica, Lambert Glacier flows into an ice shelf, and altogether is over 400 miles (650 km) long. Antarctica's Ross Ice Shelf is the world's largest sheet of floating ice. It is about as big as France!

▽ Working scientists are the only people who live in Antarctica. They try not to spoil the continent, which is protected by an international treaty. Greenpeace, shown here, keeps a check on this. At a research station at the South Pole scientists learn about living in freezing conditions.

Time

When we are trying to find things out, time is very important. Scientists often need to measure how long it takes for things to happen.

The first clocks and calendars were invented thousands of years ago. They were based on the Earth's movements. We call one spin of the Earth a day. And we call the time it takes for the Earth to travel around the Sun a year. Our time is based on these movements.

▽ **The Earth** is divided into 24 time zones, one for each hour of the day. When it's 7 AM in New York City, USA, it's noon in London, UK, and already 9 PM in Tokyo, Japan.

△ **The sundial** is a type of shadow clock. The pointer's shadow moves around the dial as the Earth spins, pointing to the time. To us, it seems as if the Sun is moving across the sky.

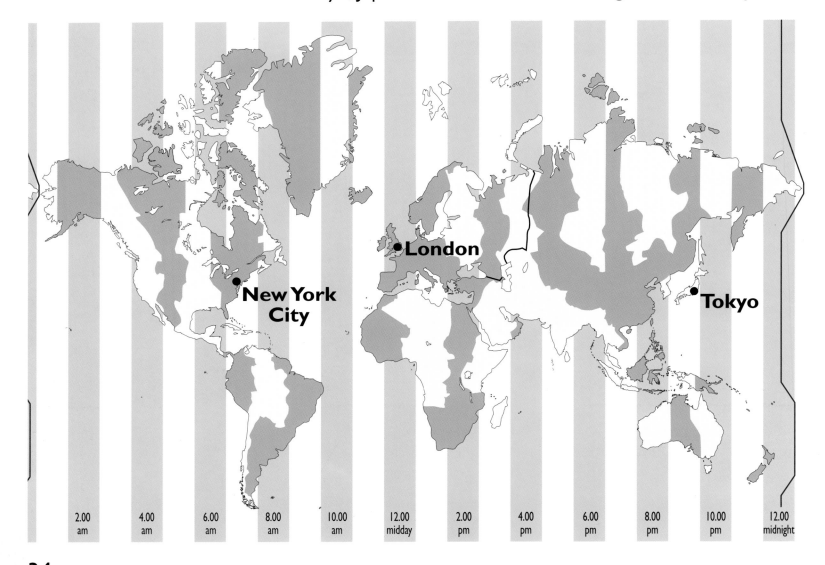

●London

●New York City

●Tokyo

| 2.00 am | 4.00 am | 6.00 am | 8.00 am | 10.00 am | 12.00 midday | 2.00 pm | 4.00 pm | 6.00 pm | 8.00 pm | 10.00 pm | 12.00 midnight |

digital watch

candle clock

grandfather clock

pocket watch

▽ **The Earth** takes a year to travel around the Sun. We split this up into 12 calendar months of, usually, 30 or 31 days.

▽ **The Moon** makes 12 trips around the Earth during a year. These are called lunar months, but do not add up exactly to one year. Muslims follow a lunar month.

WATER CLOCK

Make a small hole in the bottom of a yogurt container. Attach a length of string to the pot and hang it up. Put another yogurt container under it. Then pour water into the hanging pot. Use a watch to time a minute and mark the water level on the bottom pot with a permanent marker. Carry on timing and marking more minutes. Then empty the bottom pot and refill the hanging pot. The marks on your water clock will now show you the passing minutes.

NEW WORDS

🕐 **calendar** A chart that shows us the days, weeks, and months of the year.

🕐 **Muslim** To do with the religion of Muslim people, called Islam.

🕐 **candle clock** A candle marked to show the passing of hours.

Solids, Liquids, and Gases

Everything in the Universe, from the tiniest speck of dust to the biggest giant star, is made up of matter. This matter can take one of three forms: solid, liquid, or gas.

A solid is a piece of matter that has a definite shape. Wood is a hard solid, and rubber is a soft solid. A liquid, such as water or lemonade, does not have a definite shape, but takes the shape of its container. A gas, such as air, also has no shape, and spreads out to fill any container it is put in.

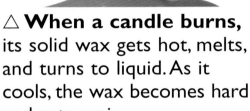

△ **When a candle burns,** its solid wax gets hot, melts, and turns to liquid. As it cools, the wax becomes hard and sets again.

▷ **Red-hot lava** comes shooting out of a volcano as a liquid. The lava cools and turns into solid rock. Whether the lava is liquid or solid depends on its temperature. This is the same with candle wax.

▽ **Concrete** is shaped when it is runny, and then it hardens. A solid concrete building cannot turn into a liquid again.

▽ **A cake is baked** from a runny mixture, but you can't change it back again.

▽ **You can fry** a runny raw egg until it goes solid, but you can't unfry it!

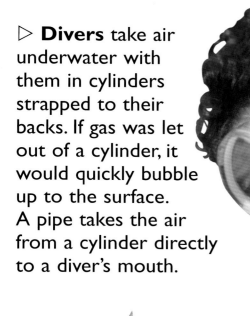

▷ **Divers** take air underwater with them in cylinders strapped to their backs. If gas was let out of a cylinder, it would quickly bubble up to the surface. A pipe takes the air from a cylinder directly to a diver's mouth.

SLOW FREEZER

Salty water does not freeze as easily as fresh water. To test this, dissolve as much salt as you can in a tin-foil container of cold tap water. Then put this in the freezer, along with another container of cold tap water. You will find that the fresh water turns to solid ice much faster than the salty water. This is because the salty water freezes at a much lower temperature.

Can water flow uphill?
No, water always flows downhill. This is because it is pulled by the force of gravity, just like everything else. Water settles at the lowest point it can reach.

NEW WORDS
🕯 **concrete** Cement mixed with sand and gravel, used in building.
🕯 **dissolve** To mix a solid into a liquid so that it becomes part of the liquid.
🕯 **steam** The very hot gas that boiling water turns into.

△ **If you pour water** into an ice cube tray and put it in the freezer, the liquid becomes solid ice. If you then heat the ice cubes, they

become liquid again. When the water boils, it turns to a gas called steam. And when the steam cools on a mirror, it changes back to water!

All living things on Earth get their energy from the Sun. The food chain shows how we use the Sun's energy. Grass and other plants turn the Sun's rays into food, so they can grow. Cows eat grass and use its energy to make milk, which we collect. When we drink the milk, we can use its energy to work, play, run, and jump!

▽ **The hot water in a radiator** warms the air, which in turn warms us. This movement of heat energy is called convection.

▽ **The Sun heats** the Earth and us by radiation. On a summer's day, it is best to stay in the shade and drink a lot to stay cool.

▽ **When you hold a hot mug,** the drink's heat passes through the mug and warms your hands. The mug is said to conduct heat.

Energy

All the world's actions and movements are caused by energy. Light, heat, and electricity are all forms of energy. Our human energy comes from food.

Energy exists in many forms, and it always changes from one form to another. A car's energy comes from gasoline. When it is burned in a car, it gives out heat energy. This turns into movement energy to make the car go. Many machines are powered in this way by fuel.

plant and animal remains

oil layer

oil well

NEW WORDS

fuel Stored energy used to power machines.

gasoline A liquid made from crude oil, used to power cars and other machines.

radiator A device in the home that gives off heat. It is often part of a central heating system.

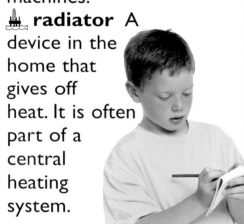

▷ **Millions of years ago**, the remains of dead sea plants and animals were covered by mud and sand. Heat and pressure turned these into oil, which was trapped between rocks. We drill down to the oil and bring it to the surface. We make gasoline from the oil, which we put into our cars. Then stored energy is turned into movement.

What a shower!
We can save energy in the home by not wasting electricity or gas. Heating water takes up energy, and a shower uses less hot water than a bath. So when we shower, we save energy.

The Sun gives off light energy from 93 million miles (150 million km) away. This is known as solar power. It is the source of all the world's energy, and it can be collected directly by solar panels and turned into electricity.

fuel tanker

service station

Electricity

Imagine what life would be like without the form of energy called electricity. You would not be able to make light or heat by flicking on a switch, and most of the machines in your home would not work!

The electricity we use at home is made in power stations. These can be powered by water, nuclear reactors, or fuel like coal, oil, or natural gas. The electricity flows through wires from the power station to our homes. We call this flow an electric current. When you turn on a light switch, a current flows to the bulb and makes it work.

◁ **Another form of electricity** does not flow through wires. It is usually still, or "static." Static electricity from a special generator can make your hair stand on end! You may have noticed this sometimes when your hair is combed quickly, especially on a cold, dry day.

NEW WORDS

⚡**amber** A hard yellow substance from the sap of ancient conifer trees.
⚡**current** The flow of electricity along a wire.
⚡**power station** A building where electricity is produced.
⚡**static** Still, not flowing as an electric current.
⚡**charge** Electricity that has been stored up.

⚡**Batteries** make and store small amounts of electricity. They are useful because you can carry them around. A car battery is very big. A flashlight battery is smaller. The battery in a watch is tiny.

WARNING!
Never touch or play with plugs, sockets, wires, or any other form of electricity. You will get an electric shock and this could kill you.

40

A flash of lightning makes a booming noise—thunder. We always hear this after we see the flash, because light travels much faster than sound.

An ancient Greek scientist named Thales discovered static electricity over 2,500 years ago, when he rubbed a piece of amber with a cloth.

△ **Lightning** is a form of static electricity. The electricity builds up inside storm clouds, and then jumps from cloud to cloud or from the cloud to the ground as brilliant flashes of lightning.

The American scientist and statesman, Benjamin Franklin, found out in 1752 that lightning is electricity. He did a famous and extremely dangerous experiment by flying a kite into a thunder cloud.

STATIC BALLOONS
Blow up a balloon and rub it up and down on a shirt. The rubbing makes static electricity on the plastic skin of the balloon. Hold the balloon against your clothes and let go. The static electricity will stick it there. You can also use the static to pick up small pieces of tissue paper. What happens when the static charge wears off?

SPINNING COLORS

Here's a way to mix the colors of the rainbow back together. Divide a cardboard disk into seven equal sections. Color the sections with the seven colors of the rainbow. Push a sharpened pencil through the middle of the disk and spin it fast on the pencil point. The colors will all mix back to a grayish white.

◁ **Light bounces off** still water in the same way that it bounces back to you from a mirror. The image that we see in the water or in a mirror is called a reflection.

Shadows are dark shapes. They are made when something gets in the way of light and blocks it out. This happens because light travels in straight lines and cannot bend around corners.

NEW WORDS

lens A curved piece of glass or plastic that is used to change the direction of light.

prism A triangular piece of glass that breaks up the colors of light.

reflection The image of something that is seen in a mirror or another reflecting surface.

triangular Having three sides, like a triangle.

In this book, all the colors you see are made of a mixture of just four colored printing inks— blue, red, yellow, and black.

▷ **If you pass a beam of light** through a triangular piece of glass, called a prism, the light gets split up into its different colors, just like a rainbow. The band of rainbow colors is called the spectrum of light.

Light and Color

Light is the fastest moving form of energy. Sunlight travels to Earth through space as light waves. We see things when light reflected from them travels to our eyes.

Light seems to us to be colorless, but really it is a mixture of colors. These are soaked up differently by various objects. A banana lets yellow bounce off it and soaks up the other colors, so the banana looks yellow.

△ **Light normally travels** in straight lines. The plastic lenses in glasses change the direction of light and help people who need them to see things more clearly.

△ **The curved lens** in a magnifying glass also bends light, making things look bigger. You can move the position of the glass, to see things the size you want.

◁ **A rainbow** shows sunlight in seven different colors. This happens when sunlight passes through raindrops and gets split up. Starting with the outer circle, the colors of a rainbow are red, orange, yellow, green, blue, indigo and violet. The colors are always in the same order.

Sound

All sounds are made by things vibrating, or moving backward and forward very quickly. Sounds travel through the air in waves.

Our ears pick up sound waves traveling in the air around us. Sounds can move through other gases too, as well as through liquids and solids. So you can hear sounds when you swim underwater. Astronauts on the Moon, where there is no air, cannot speak to each other directly and have to use radio.

LOUD AND QUIET

Bigger vibrations make bigger sound waves and sound louder. We measure loudness in decibels. Leaves falling gently on the ground might make 10 decibels of noise. A jet plane taking off makes about 120 decibels.

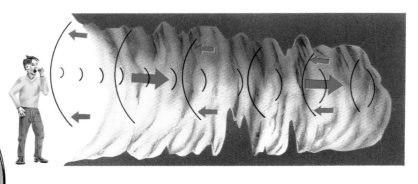

◁ **Sometimes sound waves** bounce back to you off a hard surface. When this happens, the sound makes an echo. A cave or a long corridor are good places to make an echo.

◁ **When you pluck a guitar string,** it vibrates very fast and makes sound waves. If you put your finger gently on a plucked string, you will be able to feel it vibrating. If you press down hard on the string and stop the vibration, you will also stop the sound.

Sound moves at a speed of about 740 mph (1,200 km/h). That's 30 times quicker than the fastest human runner, but almost a million times slower than the speed of light! A Concorde supersonic jet can fly at twice the speed of sound.

HIGH AND LOW

A big horn makes lower sounds than a high-pitched whistle. A big cat makes a booming roar, while a mouse makes a high-pitched squeak. That's because they make different vibrations. The quicker something vibrates, the higher the sound it makes.

whistle

horn

tiger

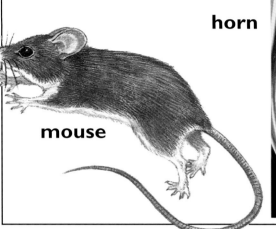

mouse

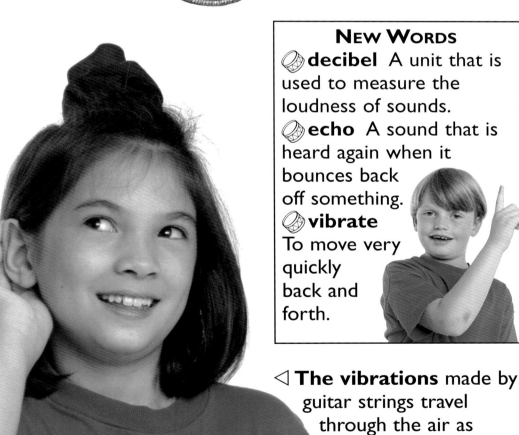

NEW WORDS

decibel A unit that is used to measure the loudness of sounds.

echo A sound that is heard again when it bounces back off something.

vibrate To move very quickly back and forth.

◁ **The vibrations** made by guitar strings travel through the air as sound waves. They do this by making the air vibrate as well. Sometimes people put a hand to their ear to try and collect more sounds.

Dogs can hear both lower and higher sounds than people can. Bats and dolphins can make and hear even higher-pitched sounds, and they use this ability to find their way around.

Why wear ear muffs?
People who work with loud machines wear muffs to protect their hearing. This is because loud noises are painful to the ears and can damage them, especially if the noise goes on for a long time.

Computers

Computers can do all sorts of different jobs for us, easily and very quickly. Many people use computers at home, as well as at work and at school.

We can use computers to write letters and reports, store lots of information—such as lists or addresses—do complicated sums, or design things.

Most of the work you do on a computer can be seen on its screen. If you want to, you can also print work out on paper.

▽ **You can use a keyboard** and a mouse to put information into the computer. Then you can store your work on a disk, as well as inside the computer itself.

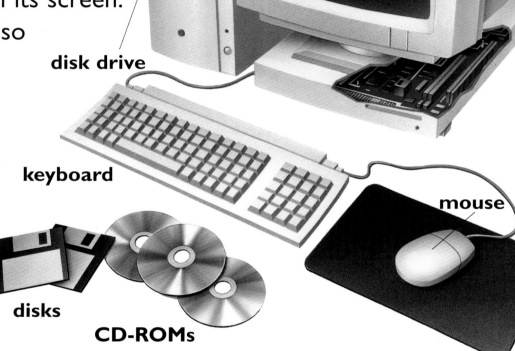

screen

disk drive

keyboard

mouse

disks

CD-ROMs

What is e-mail?

It stands for electronic mail, a way of sending messages between computers all over the world. You write a letter on your computer, then send it down a telephone line to someone else's computer, instantly. In comparison, ordinary post is so slow that e-mailers call it "snail mail."

STRINGING ALONG

To make your own phone system, make a hole in the bottom of two plastic or paper cups, or yogurt containers. Then thread a long piece of string through the holes and tie a knot at each end, inside the cup. Ask a friend to pull the string tight and put a cup to his ear. Now speak into your cup and he will hear you. It's as fast as e-mail.

▷ **There are lots** of exciting computer games. You play many of them by using a joystick.

▽ **When you put on** a virtual-reality headset, you enter a pretend world created by a computer.

Inside the headset are two small screens, showing you pictures that look real. If you use a special glove to touch things, the computer reacts to every move you make. This picture shows how the system could be used to control planes. An air traffic controller could see the planes as if they were real and give commands to tell them what to do.

TV and Radio

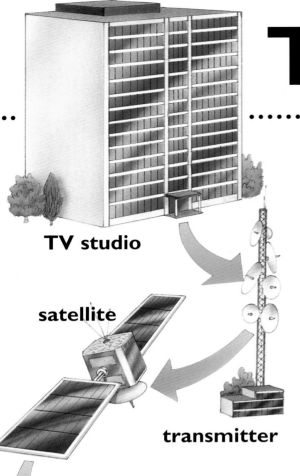

TV studio

satellite

transmitter

dish

pictures are seen in our home

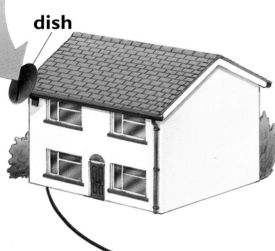

Many people spend hours each day watching TV or listening to the radio. Along with newspapers and magazines, TV and radio provide us with entertainment and information.

Television signals can be received by an antenna or by a satellite dish. Some people have TV signals brought straight into their homes through a cable. In most countries there are many different channels and programs to choose from, day and night.

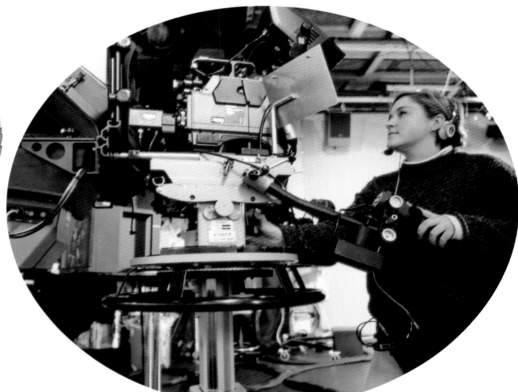

◁ **For satellite TV**, a program is transmitted to a satellite in space. The signal is then beamed back to Earth by the satellite and is picked up by dishes on people's homes. Their television set changes the signal back into pictures.

△ **Working in a TV studio,** camera operators use video cameras to record programs. These are bigger, more complicated versions of the camcorders that people use at home. Many different technicians work in TV and radio.

NEW WORDS

aerial A metal device that receives and sends TV and radio signals.

satellite dish A round aerial that receives TV signals bounced back from a satellite in space.

signal A series of radio waves that can make up pictures and sounds.

transmitter A device, usually a tall pole, that sends out radio and television signals.

△ **A TV set** receives electrical signals, which it changes into pictures. It fires streams of particles onto the back of the screen. They build up a picture, and this changes many times each second.

▽ **South Korea** makes more color television sets than any other country: over 16 million every year!

▽ **A radio telescope** is used to send and receive radio waves. Both radio and TV signals travel as radio waves. Astronomers also use radio telescopes to pick up signals from parts of space that we can't see through other telescopes.

▽ **The largest radio telescope** in the world is at Arecibo, on the Caribbean island of Puerto Rico. The dish is 1,000 feet (305 m) across and stands inside a circle of hills.

▽ **The world's first radio broadcast** was made in the USA in 1906. The first proper TV service began in 1936 in London. At that time there were just 100 television sets in the whole of the UK!

▽ **The leaves** and flowers of water lilies float on the surface of the water. We call these lily pads. The plants' stems are under the water, and their roots are in the mud and soil at the bottom of the pond.

▷ **Some bromeliads** live on other plants, in the rainforest. They grow in pockets of soil that form in the bark of trees. Their roots dangle freely and take in most of their moisture from the damp forest air.

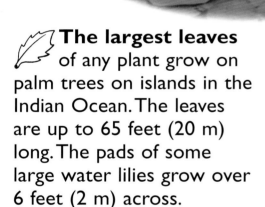

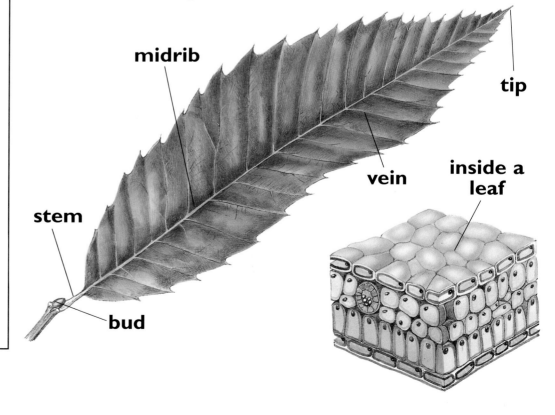

The largest leaves of any plant grow on palm trees on islands in the Indian Ocean. The leaves are up to 65 feet (20 m) long. The pads of some large water lilies grow over 6 feet (2 m) across.

▽ **Leaves** take in carbon dioxide gas through tiny holes on their underside. They also give out oxygen, which is why plants are so important to all other living creatures, including us.

△ **Cacti** live in hot, dry regions, such as deserts. They store water in their fleshy stems. Their leaves are in the shape of sharp spines, which help protect them from desert animals.

midrib

tip

stem

vein

inside a leaf

bud

Plants

Living plants are found almost everywhere on Earth where there is sunlight, warmth and water. They use these to make their own food.

Plants have a special way of using the Sun's energy, with a green substance in their leaves called chlorophyll. They take in a gas called carbon dioxide from the air and mix it with water and minerals from the soil. In this way they make a form of sugar, which is their food. This whole process is called photosynthesis.

flower

leaf

fruit

stem

roots

▷ **A plant's roots** grow down into the soil. They are covered in tiny hairs, which take in water and minerals. Water moves through the stem to the leaves, which make the plant's food.

◁ **Part of a fern** seen through a microscope. There are about 10,000 different kinds of ferns in the world. Most of these green plants are quite small.

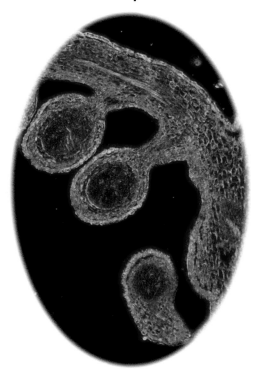

SUN BLOCK

Cover a patch of green grass with an old can or saucer—but not on someone's prize lawn! Lift the can after a few days and you will see that the grass is losing its color. After a week, it will be very pale. This is because it couldn't make food in the dark. Take the tin away and the grass will soon recover.

Trees

Trees are not only among the largest living things on Earth, but also can live the longest.

A trunk is really just a hard, woody stem. Under the protective bark, water and food travel up through the outer layer of wood, called the sapwod, to the tree's crown of branches and leaves.

Fine roots take in the water, but trees have big, strong roots as well. These will help anchor the trees very firmly in the ground.

The oldest living trees on Earth are bristlecone pines in the U.S. Southwest. Some are over 5,000 years old.

Mangrove trees grow in swamps. They are the only trees that live in salty water.

▽ **The leaves of birch trees** are shaped like triangles, with toothed edges. In the autumn, they turn brown before falling from the tree. Native Americans used the bark of birch trees to make canoes.

▽ **Different leaves** do different jobs. Small leaves, like those on fir trees or cacti, lose less water than broad, flat leaves. Big leaves show a larger surface area to the Sun and so are able to make more food.

△ **The beautiful leaves** of the tamarind, an evergreen tree that grows in warm regions of the world. It can grow to a height of 80 feet (24 m)

◁ **As an oak tree grows** and the trunk widens, its bark breaks up into pieces like a jigsaw puzzle. In the middle is a core of dark brown heartwood.

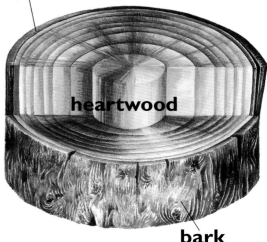

growth ring

heartwood

bark

△ **Trees grow** a new ring of wood every year. If there is lots of sunshine and rainfall, that year's ring is wide. Foresters count the rings of felled trees to see how old they are.

Many palm trees have no branches. Instead, they have large, fan-shaped leaves that grow straight out from the top of the trunk. Palms grow best in parts of the world where it is warm all year round.

BARK PATTERNS

Every tree has a unique pattern on its bark. You can see these wonderful patterns by transferring them to paper. Just attach or hold a sheet of paper firmly against a tree trunk. Then carefully rub over the paper with a crayon until the bark pattern shows up. Bark rubbings make beautiful pictures, and you can use different colored crayons to make unusual effects.

Parts of the Body

head

hand

neck

arm

torso

leg

foot

Men and women, boys and girls are all human beings. Our bodies are all similar, though no two people look exactly the same.

The human body is made up of many parts, each having its own special job to do. These different parts are all controlled by the brain, which also enables us to think and move. Our senses of sight, hearing, touch, taste, and smell help us in our daily lives. Our bodies need energy to make it work, which we get from our food.

Two thirds of your body's weight is made up of water. It also contains carbon, calcium, and iron.

◁ **The largest part** of the body is called the torso, or trunk. The four limbs are joined to the torso. The hands at the ends of our arms help us touch and hold things. Our feet help us stand upright and walk. The head is on top of the neck, which can bend and twist. The brain is inside the head.

NEW WORDS
brain The control center of the body, which also lets us think.
limb An arm or a leg.
nucleus The central part of a cell.
tissue Groups of similar cells that are joined together to form parts of the body.
torso The trunk of the human body, from below the neck to the top of the legs.

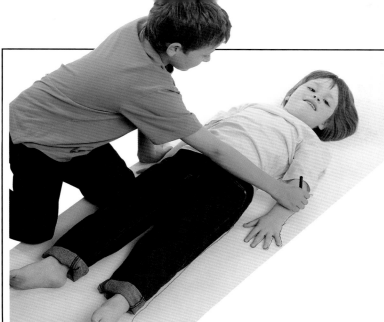

BODY SHAPES

To draw body shapes, you need some very big pieces of paper. Put the paper on the floor and ask a friend to lie on it. Draw around him or her with a pencil. Then take the paper away and cut out the outline shape. You can draw on a face and any other features you want, before pinning the picture up on the wall. Then you could ask a friend to draw your shape.

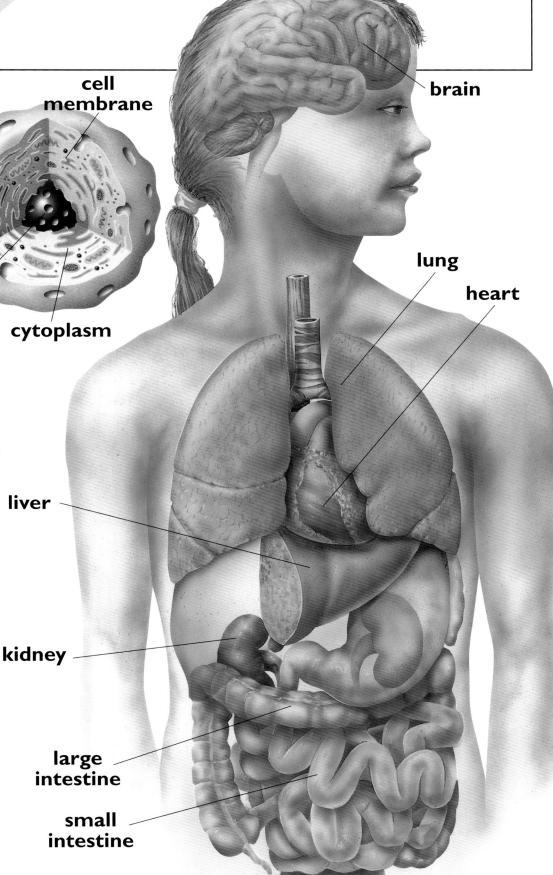

brain

cell membrane

nucleus

cytoplasm

lung

heart

liver

kidney

large intestine

small intestine

▷ **All parts of the body** are made up of tiny living units called cells. Every body contains billions of cells, so small that they can only be seen through a microscope. Most cells have three main parts. In the middle is a nucleus, the control center that helps make new cells. This is surrounded by a soft fluid called cytoplasm. The outer surface of the cell is called its membrane.

We all begin life as one single cell. This divides into two, these cells also divide, and so on. Similar types of cells join together to make tissue.

▷ **We have many large organs** inside our bodies. These are parts that do special jobs for the rest of the body. Organs work together to make up different body systems.

55

Skeleton

The skeleton is our framework of bones. Our bones provide a firm surface for muscles to attach to, helping us to move.

The skeleton also protects our body's organs. The skull protects the brain. Our heart and lungs are protected by the rib cage. The body's bones vary in shape and size. The places where they meet are called joints, which is where muscles move bones.

skull

humerus

rib

vertebra

ulna

pelvis

radius

◁ **At the center** of bones is soft marrow. This is inside the toughest part, called compact bone, which is lined with spongy bone. A bone's outer layer is called the periosteum.

spongy bone **marrow** **compact bone**

periosteum

femur

NEW WORDS
🕮 **joint** The place where two bones meet, which allows them to move.
🕮 **periosteum** The outer layer of a bone.
🕮 **skull** The framework of bones of the head.
🕮 **vertebra** One of the separate bones that make up the backbone.

▷ **33 vertebrae** make up our spine, or backbone. At the bottom is the pelvis. A woman's pelvis is wider than a man's, to make room for a baby. The lower parts of our arms and legs have two bones. The femur, or thigh bone, is the largest bone in the body.

tibia

fibula

MOVING JOINTS

Joints let us move in different ways. The hip and shoulder are ball-and-socket joints. The knee and elbow are hinge joints. There is a pivot joint at the top of the spine, a saddle joint at the thumb's base.

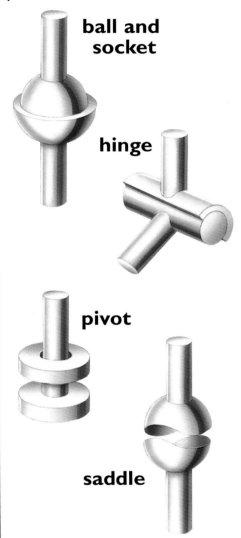

ball and socket

hinge

pivot

saddle

An adult has about 206 bones. Babies are born with as many as 270 small, soft bones. As a child grows, some of the bones join together.

You may be up to half an inch shorter in the evening than early in the morning. The weight of your upper body squashes your spine slightly as you stand and walk during the day.

▽ **For broken bones** to heal properly, they have to be placed next to each other and kept still. That is why a doctor puts a broken arm or leg in a plaster cast. New bone tissue grows to join the broken bone ends together again.

△ **Insects,** such as this beetle, have their skeleton on the outside of their body. It acts like a shell, covering and protecting the soft parts underneath. It also protects the insect from its enemies.

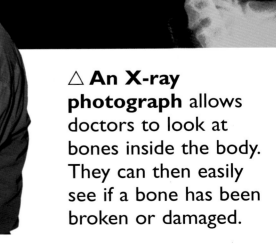

△ **An X-ray photograph** allows doctors to look at bones inside the body. They can then easily see if a bone has been broken or damaged.

Muscles

All our movements, from running and jumping, to blinking and smiling, are made by our muscles. The muscles do this by becoming shorter and pulling the bones to which they are attached.

The human body has about 620 muscles that it uses for movement. In addition there are many more that work automatically. These include the muscles that make the heart beat, the chest muscles that help us breathe, and the stomach muscles that help us digest food.

chest muscles

biceps

abdominal muscles

sartorius

NEW WORDS
buttocks The two rounded parts that form the backside, or bottom.
digest To eat and break down food so that it can provide energy for the body.
rib cage Framework of bones, or ribs, that surrounds the chest.

▷ **The body** is moved by several layers of muscles. There are large muscles near the surface under the skin, and others lie beneath them. Three layers of criss-crossing abdominal muscles connect the rib cage to the pelvis. The body's largest muscle is in the buttock.

▽ **More than 30 small muscles** run from the skull to the skin. These allow us to make facial expressions, which we use to show our feelings.

happy

sad

shocked

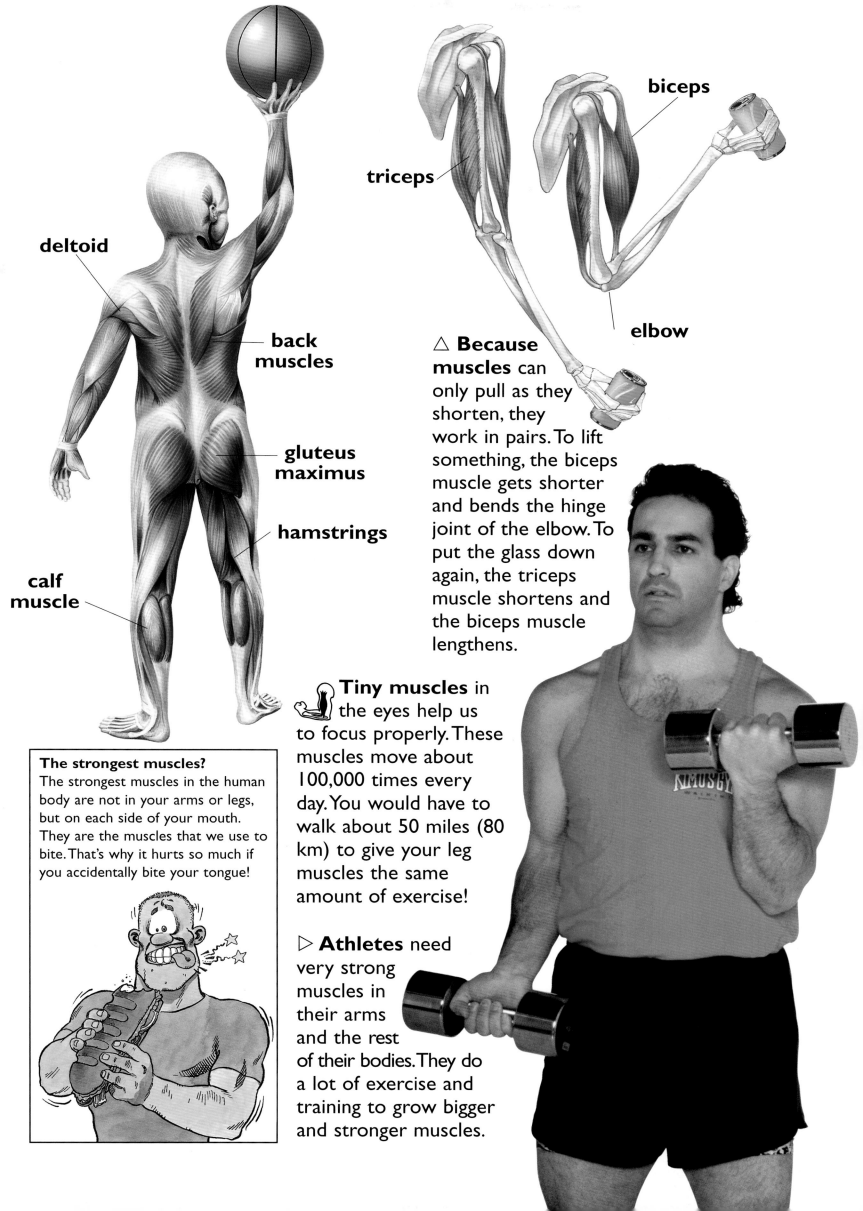

deltoid

back muscles

gluteus maximus

hamstrings

calf muscle

triceps

biceps

elbow

△ **Because muscles** can only pull as they shorten, they work in pairs. To lift something, the biceps muscle gets shorter and bends the hinge joint of the elbow. To put the glass down again, the triceps muscle shortens and the biceps muscle lengthens.

Tiny muscles in the eyes help us to focus properly. These muscles move about 100,000 times every day. You would have to walk about 50 miles (80 km) to give your leg muscles the same amount of exercise!

▷ **Athletes** need very strong muscles in their arms and the rest of their bodies. They do a lot of exercise and training to grow bigger and stronger muscles.

The strongest muscles?
The strongest muscles in the human body are not in your arms or legs, but on each side of your mouth. They are the muscles that we use to bite. That's why it hurts so much if you accidentally bite your tongue!

The Heart and Blood Circulation

The heart is a powerful muscle that pumps blood all around the body. The blood carries oxygen from the air we breathe and goodness from the food we eat.

The heart is pear-shaped and is about as big as your clenched fist. It lies in your chest, behind your ribs and just to the left of the bottom of your breastbone. If you put your hand on your chest near your heart, you can feel it beating. A child's heart rate is about 100 beats a minute. When you are running or if you are very active, your heart beats faster and your body's cells then need more oxygen and food.

heart

artery

vein

Hold one hand up and the other down for one minute.

△ **Blood** travels away from the heart in blood vessels called arteries. It travels back to the heart in veins. In the illustration, arteries are red and veins blue.

▷ **Your heart** has to work harder to pump blood upward, because then it is working against gravity. If you hold one hand up for a minute, you'll see that it has less blood in it afterward than the other hand.

60

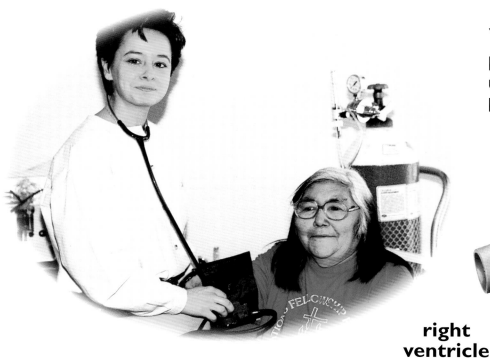

▽ **The right side** of the heart pumps blood to the lungs to pick up oxygen. The left side pumps the blood around the body.

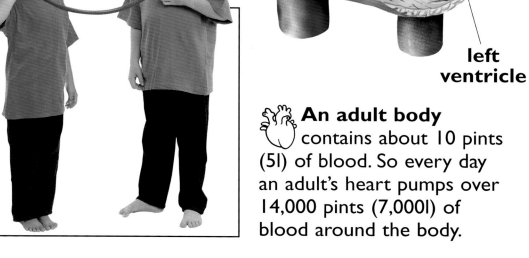

aorta

right ventricle

left ventricle

△ **A doctor** can use a special instrument to measure blood pressure. The instrument squeezes, but it isn't painful. Having high blood pressure can put an extra strain on a person's heart. because it has to work harder.

LISTEN TO THE BEAT

You can make your own stethoscope, so that you can easily listen to your own or a friend's heartbeat. Simply cut the top end off two plastic bottles. Then push the ends of some plastic tubing into these two cups. Put one cup over a friend's heart and the other cup over your ear.

An adult body contains about 10 pints (5l) of blood. So every day an adult's heart pumps over 14,000 pints (7,000l) of blood around the body.

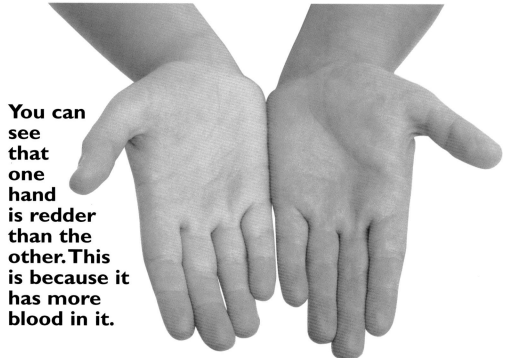

You can see that one hand is redder than the other. This is because it has more blood in it.

NEW WORDS

artery One of the tubes that carries blood away from the heart to all parts of the body.

stethoscope A doctor's instrument used for listening to sounds in a person's body.

vein One of the tubes that carries blood to the heart.

◁ **Runners** need to get a lot of oxygen to their muscles very quickly. To achieve this, they breathe hard and their hearts beat quicker. That's why you sometimes feel out of breath when you've been running.

An adult's lungs contain around 300 billion tiny blood vessels, called capillaries. If laid end to end, they would stretch over 1,200 miles (2,000 km).

We can't breathe underwater, so divers carry oxygen tanks on their backs. On the surface, they use snorkels. There is no air in space, so astronauts also carry backpacks of oxygen.

△ **This photo** of part of a lung was taken under a microscope, which magnifies it many times. The network of small passages inside the lung make it look and act rather like a sponge.

▷ **As you breathe in,** your rib cage expands and a large dome of muscle, called the diaphragm, flattens. When you breathe out, the diaphragm rises.

BREATH TEST

Fill a large plastic bottle and half-fill a large bowl with water. Cover the bottletop with your finger and turn it upside down in the bowl. You will find that the water will stay in the bottle. Take a plastic tube and carefully put one end of it into the neck of the bottle, under the water. Now everything is ready for the breath test. Blow hard into the free end of the tube. How much water can your breath push out of the bottle?

Breathing

Every time we breathe, we take in air containing a gas called oxygen. We need oxygen all the time to make our bodies work.

The air we breathe in passes into the two lungs, which are well protected inside the rib cage. The lungs take oxygen from the air and pass it into our bloodstream. Our blood takes oxygen all around the body.

When we breathe out, the lungs get rid of used air. Adults breathe about 18 times a minute, which is more than 25,000 times a day. Children usually breathe even faster.

nasal cavity

mouth — windpipe

rib cage

bronchial tube

lung

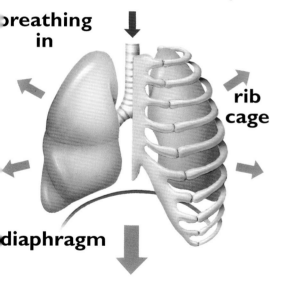

breathing in

rib cage

diaphragm

breathing out

▽ **People who suffer from asthma,** or other breathing difficulties, often use an inhaler to help them breathe. The inhaler puffs a drug down into the windpipe. This makes the air passages wider and they can breathe more easily.

△ **The air we breathe** in through the nose and mouth goes down the windpipe. This branches into two bronchial tubes, one for each lung. Inside the lungs, the tubes divide and get smaller.

Oxygen passes from the tiniest tubes to blood vessels and finally into the bloodstream.

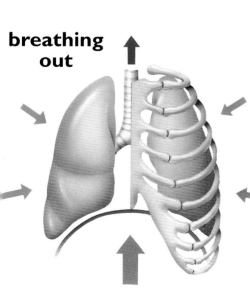

Central Nervous System

A network of nerves runs throughout your whole body. These nerves carry instructions from the brain, as well as messages from your sense organs back to the brain.

The nerves branch off from the spinal cord, which is connected to the brain. Together they make up the body's central nervous system. The brain is the body's control center. It tells the rest of the body what to do.

△ **If you tap** the right point below someone's knee, his or her leg will jerk. This is called a reflex action. The spinal cord sends a signal back to the leg muscle before the original message has reached the brain.

Reflex actions help the body to protect itself quickly. So if you touch a sharp pin or something hot, you will pull your hand away before the message reaches your brain without thinking about it.

Left or right?
The left half of the brain controls the right side of the body, while the right half looks after the left side. Very few people can write or draw well with both hands. Try using your "wrong" hand, to see how hard it is.

NEW WORDS

central nervous system The brain and the spinal cord.

reflex action A response by the body that takes place without the brain being involved.

spinal cord The column of nerves running to and from the brain down the middle of the backbone.

Our brain uses an enormous amount of energy. It uses about a fifth of the oxygen we breathe, as well as a fifth of the energy in the food we eat. With this it produces its own electricity.

△ **Memories** are stored in the brain. This couple will always remember their wedding day.

▷ **The brain** is connected to the spinal cord that runs down the body inside the backbone. Nerves run from the spine all over the body, even to your little toe.

◁ **Our brain** helps us to see and hear, as well as to judge speed and distance. A racing driver needs to combine all of these abilities very quickly. His brain sends messages to his hands and feet to steer and control the car.

straight hair

wavy hair

curly hair

△ **Hairs** grow from follicles, in the dermis. Different-shaped follicles make people's hair straight, wavy, or curly.

 **No two fingerprints** are the same. Every person in the world has their own special pattern. That's why fingerprints can be used to identify people.

◁ **People sweat** when they are hot, so athletes sweat more on a very hot day. Sweat takes heat from the body and helps cool you down as it dries on your skin.

COMPARE PRINTS

It's best to wear some old clothes and put down lots of newspaper for this activity. It can be a bit messy! Use a roller or a brush to cover your fingers or your whole hand in paint. Then press down firmly on a sheet of paper. This will leave fingerprints and perhaps a whole hand print. When you have finished, compare your prints with a friend's. Are the prints the same? You could try looking at them through a magnifying glass—you'll really see the difference.

The Skin, Hair, and Nails

nail

half-moon

cuticle

fat

bone

skin

Skin protects the body and controls its temperature. It keeps out dirt, water, and germs, shields us from the Sun's burning rays, and stops the body drying out.

△ **Nails** are made of a tough substance called keratin. New nail grows from the base, under the skin. The pale half-moon is nail that has just grown.

Our skin is full of nerve endings, so it can send messages to the brain about things such as heat, cold, and pain. The skin produces nails to protect the tips of fingers and toes. It also makes hairs for extra warmth and protection.

▽ **The tough outer layer** of the skin is called the epidermis, which is waterproof and germproof. The inner layer, called the dermis, contains nerve endings. This is also where hairs grow and sweat is made.

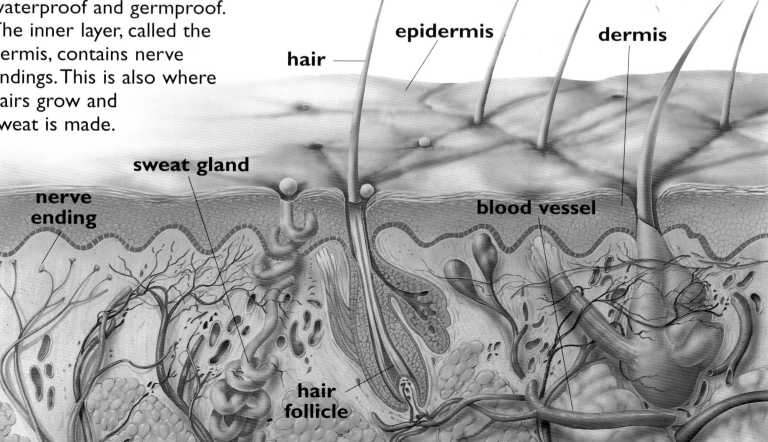

epidermis

dermis

hair

sweat gland

nerve ending

blood vessel

hair follicle

Food and Drink

We need energy to live, and we get that energy from what we eat and drink. Our bodies need important substances, called nutrients, that we get from food. They help us grow and repair damaged cells, as well as providing energy.

Different foods are useful to us in different ways. It is important that we don't miss out on any of the essential nutrients. To have a balanced diet, we must eat foods from various groups—carbohydrates, proteins, fats, and fiber, also vitamins and minerals.

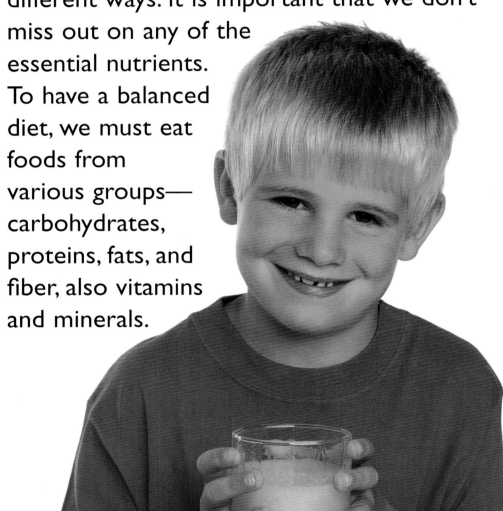

△ **Cereals and vegetables** are good to eat because they contain a lot of fiber. This is very useful because it helps other foods pass more easily through the digestive system.

The body needs small amounts of minerals, such as calcium and sodium. Calcium is needed for healthy bones and teeth. Milk contains calcium, as well as water, fat, protein, and vitamins.

◁ **Oranges** and other fruit contain a lot of Vitamin C, which keeps us healthy and helps us recover from illness. The body needs many other vitamins too.

▽ **Fats** such as cheese, butter, and milk are full of energy, as well as important vitamins. Fats can be stored by the body to use later, but it is not good to eat too many fatty foods.

NEW WORDS

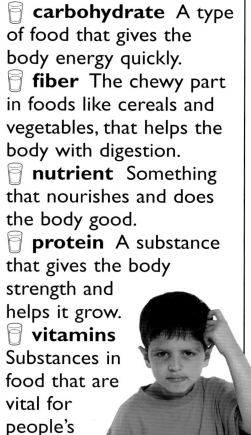

▯ **carbohydrate** A type of food that gives the body energy quickly.

▯ **fiber** The chewy part in foods like cereals and vegetables, that helps the body with digestion.

▯ **nutrient** Something that nourishes and does the body good.

▯ **protein** A substance that gives the body strength and helps it grow.

▯ **vitamins** Substances in food that are vital for people's health.

△ **Beans and meat** contain lots of proteins, which help us stay strong. They are also used to make body cells, so they help us grow and stay healthy.

▽ **Carbohydrates,** such as bread and pasta, give us a lot of the energy that we need for our daily lives. We can make use of this type of energy very quickly.

Why do we need water?
The body uses water in many ways. Water helps to make up our blood. It keeps us cool by making sweat. It carries wastes from the body in urine. We get water from other drinks too, as well as from many different kinds of food.

HOME-MADE GRANOLA

Put 2 cups oats, 3/4 cups raisins, and 1/2 cup chopped nuts, along with some sunflower seeds, in a mixing bowl. Mix all the ingredients together. Then put your granola in a screw-top jar. Label the jar, adding the date. You can eat your granola with milk, yogurt, or fresh fruit juice, and have a healthy breakfast.

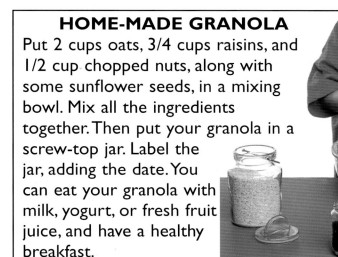

Smell and Taste

Smell and taste are important senses. Our sense of smell is much stronger than our sense of taste. When we taste food, we rely on its smell and texture to give us information about it as well.

We use our noses for smelling things. Tiny scent particles go into the nose with the air. The nose then sends messages through a nerve to the brain, which recognizes the smell.

The tongue also sends nerve signals to the brain about tastes. When we eat something, the tongue and the nose combine to let the brain know all about that particular food.

△ **Flowers** give off a pleasant scent, to attract insects. A skunk can make a very nasty smell when it wants to scare off enemies.

When you have a cold and your nose is plugged, you can't smell much and you can't taste your food properly either.

▷ **We taste different things** on different parts of the tongue. We taste sweet things at the tip, salty things just behind the tip, sour things at the sides, and bitter things at the back of the tongue.

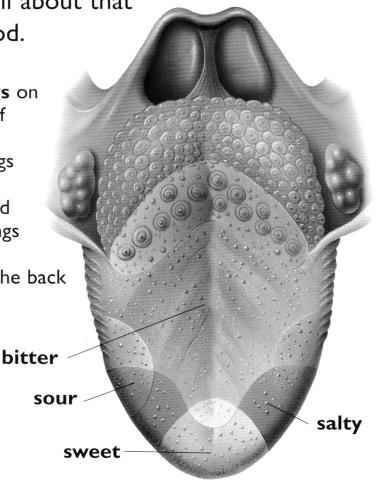

bitter

sour

sweet

salty

Why do we sneeze?
We sneeze to help clear our noses of unwanted particles, such as dust. When we sneeze, the explosive rush of air from the lungs can reach a speed of 100 mph (160 kph)—as fast as a sports car!

TASTE WITHOUT SMELL

See how much you can taste without the help of your nose. Cut an apple, a carrot, some cheese, and other foods with a similar texture into cubes. Cover your eyes and nose and ask a friend to give you the pieces one by one. Can you taste the difference? Try the test on your friend too.

Most people can identify about 3,000 different smells.

▽ **This photo** of taste buds was taken through a microscope. Our tongue has about 10,000 taste buds, which pick up the four basic tastes and pass the information on.

NEW WORDS

mucus A moist, sticky substance in the nose.

olfactory nerve A nerve that runs from the nose to the brain, taking messages about smells.

particle A very very small piece of something.

taste bud A sense organ on the tongue that helps us taste things.

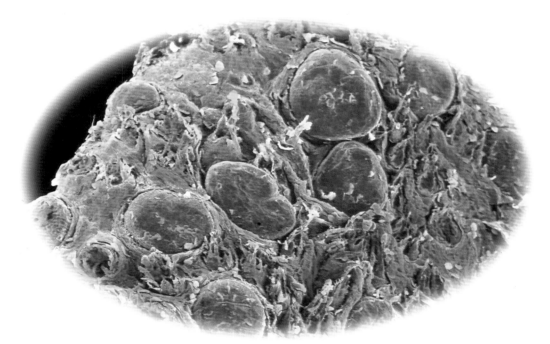

Babies have taste buds all over the inside of their mouths. They are also very sensitive to smells. As we grow older, our sense of smell gets weaker.

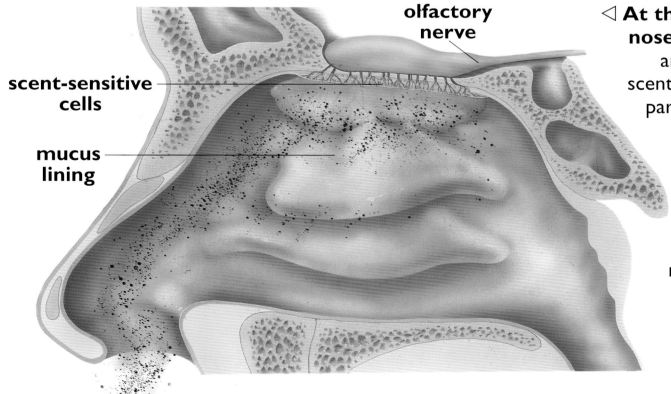

olfactory nerve

scent-sensitive cells

mucus lining

◁ **At the top of the nose** are cells that are sensitive to scent particles. The particles dissolve in a lining of mucus, and signals are sent along the olfactory nerve. This nerve leads to a special part of the brain, where smells are identified.

71

Hearing

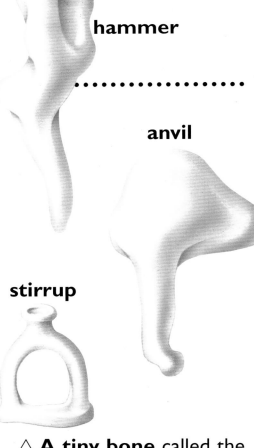

hammer

anvil

stirrup

When we look at someone's ears, we see only a part of them. This part, called the outer ear, is shaped to collect sounds as they travel through the air.

All sounds are made by things vibrating. Sound waves make the eardrums and other parts vibrate. Information on vibrations is then sent to the brain, which lets us hear the sounds.

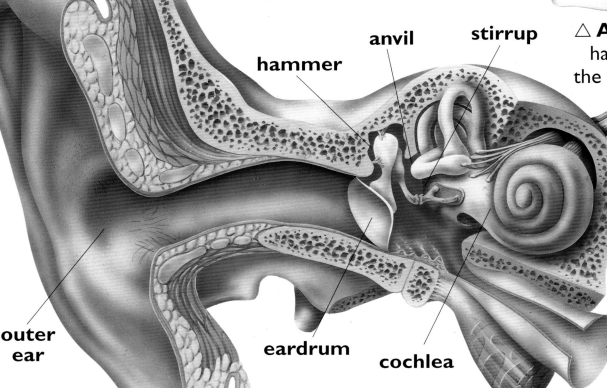

anvil

stirrup

hammer

outer ear

eardrum

cochlea

△ **A tiny bone** called the hammer is connected to the eardrum. The eardrum vibrates the hammer. The hammer then moves the anvil, which in turn moves the stirrup bone. Finally, the stirrup vibrates the cochlea.

△ **Sounds** pass into the ear and make the eardrum vibrate, which in turn vibrates tiny bones. The bones shake a spiral tube shaped like a snail shell, called the cochlea. Inside the cochlea is a fluid, which moves tiny hairs that send signals to the brain. Then we hear the sounds.

EARDRUM DRUM

To make a pretend eardrum, cut a large piece from a plastic bag. Stretch it over the top of a big can and hold it in place with a rubber band. Sprinkle some sugar onto the plastic. Then hold a metal tray near to it and hit the tray with a wooden spoon. The grains of sugar will jump about as your drum vibrates with the sound.

▽ **An old-fashioned ear trumpet** worked by acting as a bigger outer ear and making sounds louder. Modern hearing aids have tiny microphones and speakers.

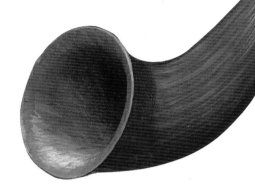

🦻 **Have you ever** felt your ears pop in a plane or an elevator? This sometimes happens when air pressure outside changes and is equalized in the middle ear.

▽ **Sounds travel well** through liquids, so it is easy to hear when you are underwater. Whales and other sea creatures make sounds to communicate with each other.

△ **Three canals** next to the cochlea, in the inner ear, help us keep our balance. They let the brain know what movements the body is making. Ballet dancers need excellent balance.

Seeing

We use our eyes to see. Rays of light come into each eye through an opening called the pupil, which is in the middle.

A lens inside each eye then bends the light very precisely, so that it travels to an area at the back of the eye called the retina.

The light rays make an image on the retina, but the image is upside down. Nerves send information on the image to the brain, which lets us see it the right way up.

▽ **Our eyes** are about the size of table-tennis balls, but we only see a small part at the front when we look in the mirror. The pupil is surrounded by a colored iris, which has a clear protective shield in front of it, called the cornea.

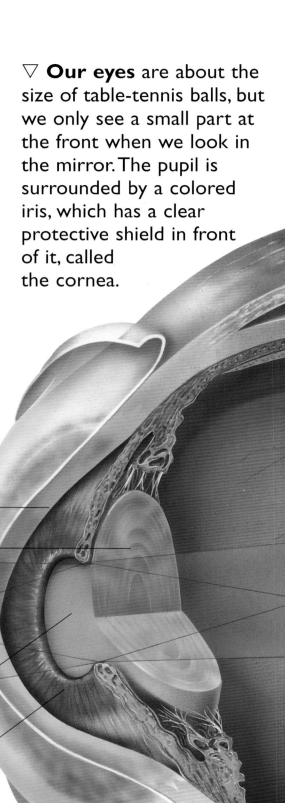

cornea

lens

pupil

iris

△ **Most people see** things in color, but some are color blind. This is a test card for color blindness. Can you see the shape inside the circle?

▷ **The color** of our eyes is really just the color of the iris. We inherit this color from our parents, and the most common color is brown. If one parent has blue eyes and the other brown, their child will usually have brown eyes.

74

▷ **Many people** wear glasses or contact lenses to help them see better. These change the direction of light before it enters the eyes, so that it focuses better on the retina.

Why do we blink?
Our eyes make tears all the time. Tears are useful because they keep the cornea at the front of the eye damp. When we blink, it spreads the tears across the eyes. This keeps the eyes clean and stops them from drying out.

optic nerve

retina

day

night

△ **When it is sunny or a bright day,** our eyes do not need to let in much light, and our pupils are small. But when there is less light, like at nighttime, the pupils have to open more and they get bigger. Small muscles change the size of the iris around the pupil.

NEW WORDS

👁 **cornea** The clear protective layer that covers the pupil.

👁 **iris** The colored part of the eye surrounding the pupil.

👁 **pupil** The opening at the front of the eye that lets in light.

👁 **retina** The layer at the back of the eye that is sensitive to light.

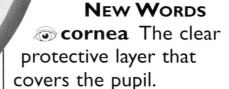

👁 **You blink** about 15 times each minute, without thinking about it. The brain controls many actions such as this automatically.

👁 **About one in every 12 men** find it very difficult to tell the difference between some colors, especially red and green. Very few women are color blind.

Mammals

There are many animals in the group we call mammals. Human beings are mammals, too. A mammal has hair or fur on its body, to help keep it warm. Baby mammals are fed with milk from their mother's body.

Mammals live all over the world, from the freezing polar regions to the hot tropics. Most mammals live on land, but whales live in the sea and bats can fly. They are known as warm-blooded animals.

△ **There are more than 400** different breeds of sheep. We shear them so that we can use their furry coats to make wool.

◁ **A porcupine** has long spines, called quills. It can raise and rattle its quills to warn off any of its enemies.

△ **Some mammals,** such as this otter, have whiskers. These help them feel things and find their way about.

◁ **Bears** are large mammals with powerful legs and strong claws. They eat plants as well as meat. They live mainly on the ground but can stand on their back legs and can even climb trees.

The largest mammal is the blue whale. The largest on land is the African elephant. The tallest is the giraffe. The fastest is the cheetah. And the smallest is the tiny hog-nosed bat.

▷ **The white rhinoceros** is one of the world's five species of rhino. They all have horns and for this reason are under threat from hunters.

△ **Kudu antelopes** have beautifully curved horns. Males sometimes use these to fight each other. Kudus live in small groups in Africa, and their main enemies are leopards, lions, and wild dogs.

NEW WORDS

★ **breed** A variety of animal.

★ **descendant** A person or animal that has come by birth from another person or animal.

★ **tropics** The hottest part of the world, which is near the Equator.

△ **Farmyard pigs** are descendants of wild boars. Farmers keep them for their meat, which we call pork, ham, and bacon. The female pig, called a sow, lies down to feed milk to all her piglets at the same time.

SNOWED IN

Female polar bears dig a den in a snowdrift in the freezing Arctic region. There they give birth to their cubs in midwinter, protecting them from the severe cold and wind. The tiny cubs stay in the den for about three months. Their mother feeds them with her own milk, though she eats nothing herself. Mother and cubs come out onto the snow and ice in spring. Mother then spends most of her time looking for food, such as seals.

Apes and Monkeys

Apes are generally larger than monkeys, and they have no tails. There are four types of ape. Gorillas and chimpanzees live only in Africa, and orangutans and gibbons live only in Southeast Asia.

Many different types of old world monkeys are found in both Africa and Asia. The new world monkeys of Central and South America have long tails, which they often use to hold on to branches as they swing through the trees.

Most apes and monkeys live in the world's rain forests, many of which are being destroyed.

△ **Male mandrills** have very colorful faces. Mandrills live in African forests, staying mainly on the ground in troops of up to 50 animals. They feed on fruit, nuts, and small animals, and sleep in trees.

▷ **Many monkeys**, such as this macaque, live together in large troops. Each troop has a leader, usually an old, strong male. They spend most of their time in trees and have good eyesight, hearing, and sense of smell.

▷ **Orangutans** live in the tropical rainforests of Borneo and Sumatra. In the Malay language, this ape's name means "man of the forest." In many places, its home is being cut down for timber. Reserves have been set up to protect it.

▽ **The gorilla** is the largest ape. Males are sometimes over 6 feet (1.8 m) tall, the same height as a tall man. They are powerful, but they are also peaceful and gentle. They rarely climb trees.

△ **Grooming** each other to get rid of irritating pests is an enjoyable group activity for these chimpanzees.

▷ **South American spider monkeys** have amazing tails which can wrap round and cling to branches.

Chimpanzees are good tool-makers. They use sticks to get honey and insects from nests, and they use stones to crack nuts.

MONKEY MOBILE
Trace the monkey (right) and cut out its shape. Draw around the shape on cardboard and cut it out. Make two more monkeys and draw on faces. Make a small hole in each monkey and tie on pieces of thread. Tie the monkeys to some rolled cardboard. When the monkeys are balanced, fix the knots with a drop of glue.

Elephants

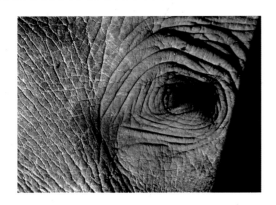

△ **Elephants** have thick, wrinkled skin. Their eyesight is not very good, but they have good hearing and an excellent sense of smell.

▷ **An elephant's tusks** are really two big teeth made of ivory. They are useful for digging and breaking off large branches. The trunk can be used to pick up food and guide it into an elephant's mouth.

▽ **Elephants love bathing.** They can give themselves a shower through their trunks and are good swimmers.

There are two species (or two different kinds), of elephant—African and Asian. The African elephant has large ears and is the world's biggest land animal. Males can grow up to 13 feet (4 m) high at the shoulder, which is over twice as tall as a man. They can weigh up to 7 tons, which is as much as 90 people! Asian elephants are smaller and lighter, with smaller ears. They live in India, Sri Lanka, and parts of Southeast Asia.

△ **A tree** is useful for scratching an annoying itch!

NEW WORDS

herd A large group of animals living together.

logging Cutting down trees to use the wood.

trunk An elephant's long, bendy nose.

tusk One of the two long pointed teeth sticking out of an elephant's mouth.

▷ **Asian elephants** are used in the logging industry, because they can move and carry very heavy loads. Riders sit behind the animal's neck. In some countries, elephants are still used as a means of getting around.

 **Elephants sometimes use** their trunks as snorkels. When they swim, they can stick their trunks upward so that they breathe in plenty of air.

Do elephants use skin care?
Yes! To prevent their skin from cracking, elephants wallow and cover themselves in cool mud. This dries on their bodies and helps protect them from the burning sun. It also gets rid of flies and ticks. An elephant's color depends on the mud it wallows in.

◁ **Elephants** can reach food high up in trees. They are vegetarians, and their diet includes leaves, fruit, bark, and roots.

Elephants live in family groups, which often join together to make large herds. Each group is led by a female elephant, who is usually the oldest. She decides which routes the herd should follow to find food and water, often traveling in single file.

Cats

There are a number of species, or different kinds, of cats. Even the biggest wild cats are relatives of our pet cats at home!

△ **Cheetahs** are the fastest cats. In fact, they are the fastest runners in the world. They can reach a speed of 60 mph (100 kph) for a short distance.

🐾 **Tigers** are the biggest cats. From head to tail they are up to 12 feet (3.6 m) long. These powerful animals make very good mothers to their baby cubs.

🐾 **Pet cats** are used to living with people, and to being fed by their owners. But sometimes they hunt, chasing after birds and mice before pouncing. While lions and tigers roar, a pet cat just meows!

All cats are carnivores. They are built to hunt, and their bodies are powerful. To help them catch their prey, cats have sharp eyesight and a good sense of smell. They can run very fast too. Their size, coloring, and coat patterns vary, but all cats have a similar shape.

▷ **Members of the cat family:** they look alike but live in different ways.

▷ **Male and female lions** look very different. The male has a big brown mane. Lions are the only cats that live together in groups, called prides. Lions like to sit around and let the lionesses do most of the hunting.

jaguar

puma

◁ **The top male** lion is challenged by other males in the pride from time to time. He has to fight them in order to keep his position as the dominant male in the group.

△ **Big cats** like flat, open country, where they can see a long way. They follow their prey until they are close enough to strike.

▷ **Pet cats** and many of the big cats don't like water. But tigers search it out during the hottest part of the day. Then they are often found cooling off in a pool. They are excellent swimmers and can easily cross rivers.

Why do leopards have spots?
Because they make leopards difficult to see. From a distance, the black spots on the yellow fur look like light on the grass or in the trees. This is called camouflage. It helps the leopard to hide from the animals it is hunting, and from those hunting it.

leopard

lynx

black panther

cheetah

lions

WHALES TO SCALE

Draw whales and dolphins in scale with each other. You can use the scale 1:144. This means using an inch for every 12 feet, so your blue whale will be 9 inches long. The whales' real lengths are: common dolphin 6 feet, bottlenose dolphin 12 feet, narwhal 20 feet, pilot whale 25 feet, killer whale 30 feet, and the blue whale 108 feet.

△ **Pilot whales**, like the one at the top of the photo, have a big, round head. They live in large groups, called schools, of hundreds or even thousands. The other dolphin is a bottlenose.

▽ **The blue whale** is the largest animal in the world. It can grow up to 108 feet (33 m) long and weigh over 150 tons. Blue whales swim in all the world's oceans, usually alone or in small groups.

△ **These common dolphins** are leaping out of the water at great speed. Most dolphins swim at about 20 mph (30 kph). This is over three times faster than even the quickest human swimmers can manage.

NEW WORDS

baleen The whalebone at the front of some whales' mouths.

blowhole The nostril on top of a whale's head, through which it breathes.

dolphinarium A pool for dolphins, where they give public displays.

school A group of fish, whales, or dolphins.

Instead of teeth, blue whales have strips of whalebone, called baleen. When the whales take in water, the baleen traps tiny shrimps called krill.

Other whales, such as killer whales and sperm whales, have teeth. Dolphins are small-toothed whales.

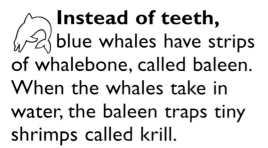

Whales and Dolphins

△ **The narwhal** is a small Arctic whale with a long tusk.

Whales and dolphins are mammals, **and they cannot breathe underwater like fish. So they come to the surface often, to take in air.**

Whales and dolphins breathe in and out through a blowhole on the top of the head. When they let out used air, they usually send out a spray of water at the same time.

△ **Some whales and dolphins** are kept in zoos and dolphinariums. Killer whales are very popular performers. They can jump as high as 16 feet (5 m).

▷ **Many whales and dolphins** live and hunt for their food in groups. They eat fish, squid, and shrimps.

blue whale

Reptiles

Snakes, lizards, and crocodiles are all reptiles. Unlike mammals, these scaly skinned animals are all cold-blooded. This means that they always need lots of sunshine to warm them up.

Reptiles are found on land and in water. Most live in warm parts of the world, and some live in hot deserts. They move into a burrow if it is too hot above ground, or if it is ever too cold in winter.

Most reptiles have four legs, but snakes are long, legless reptiles. All snakes are meat-eaters, and some kill their prey with poison from hollow teeth called fangs.

△ **Marine iguanas** are the only lizards that swim in the sea. They live around the Galapagos Islands, in the Pacific Ocean. They go to sea to feed on seaweed and then warm up on the islands' volcanic rocks.

The largest lizard is the Komodo dragon of Indonesia. It can grow up to 10 feet (3 m) long.

▽ **The horned lizard** has strong armour, to protect it from its enemies. It has pointed scales, as well as horns behind its head. It lives in dry areas and deserts of America, where it feeds mainly on ants. The female horned lizard lays her eggs in a hole in the ground.

A skink is a kind of lizard. It can make its tail fall off if when it is attacked by an enemy. This usually confuses the enemy, so that the lizard can quickly escape. It then grows a new tail.

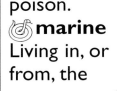

NEW WORDS

chameleon A lizard with a long tongue and the ability to change color.

fang A snake's long, pointed, hollow tooth, through which it can pass its poison.

marine Living in, or from, the sea.

▷ **Chameleons** are slow-moving, tree-living lizards. If they see an insect within range, they shoot out a long sticky tongue to catch it. They can also change color to suit their surroundings or their mood. An angry chameleon may turn black.

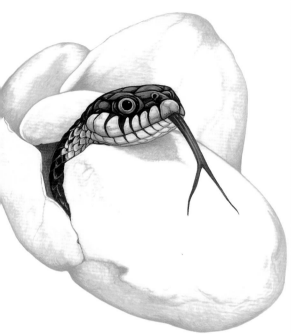

△ **Most reptiles lay eggs**, which are soft and leathery. Snakes lay their eggs in shallow holes and cover them with a thin layer of soil. When the baby snakes hatch out, they have to look after themselves.

The longest snake is the reticulated python of Southeast Asia, which grows up to 30 feet (9 m) long. The most poisonous snake is the small-scaled snake living in Australia.

▽ **Emerald tree boas** live in the rain forests of South America. They wrap themselves around branches and watch out for prey, often birds and bats. They move fast and also swim very well.

Birds

Birds are the only animals with feathers. They have wings, and most are expert fliers. There are more than 9,000 different types, living in all parts of the world.

Female birds lay eggs, and most build nests to protect them. When the eggs hatch out, the adults feed their young until the small birds can fly and leave the nest.

△ **Gulls** and other seabirds spend much of their time at sea. They glide over the water, waiting to swoop down to catch fish. Many seabirds nest on rocky cliffs.

▽ **Arctic terns** raise their young near the North Pole. Then they fly south to the Antarctic for the summer. In the fall they fly north again, making a round trip of 22,400 miles.

◁ **The Indian peacock** spreads his tail feathers into a fan. He does this to attract the female peahen.

▽ **Birds** have various beaks. With its beak, a macaw can crack nuts, a pelican scoops fish, and an eagle can tear meat.

NEW WORDS

🐦 **Arctic** The very cold continent at the top of the world, also called The North Pole.

🐦 **Antarctic** The cold continent at the bottom of the world (or South Pole).

🐦 **gull** A large seabird.

macaw

pelican

flamingo

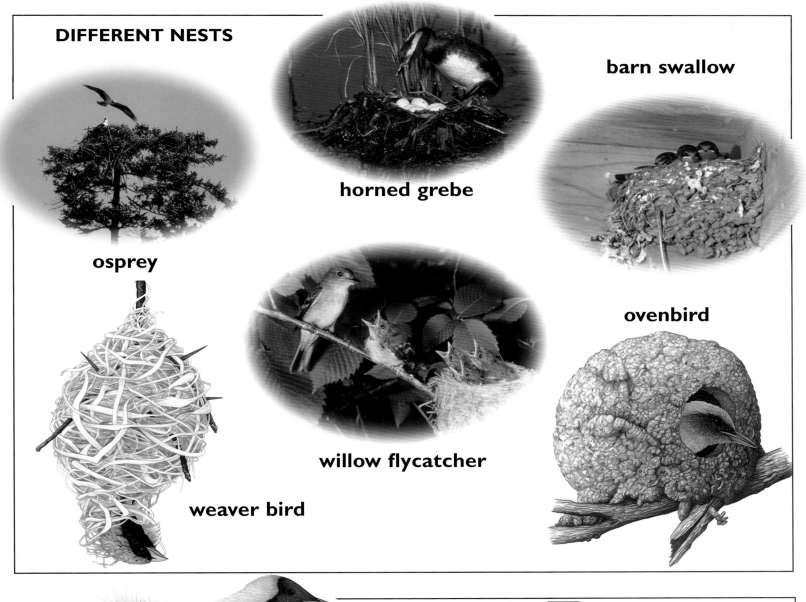

DIFFERENT NESTS

barn swallow

horned grebe

osprey

ovenbird

willow flycatcher

weaver bird

BIRD OF PARADISE

Draw a bird of paradise on blue cardboard with white crayon. Cut out pieces of colored paper to fit the head and body, and stick feather shapes on the body. Add long strips of tissue paper for the tail, and don't forget feet, a beak and a button eye. You could make a rain forest background too, with real twigs and leaves.

bird of paradise

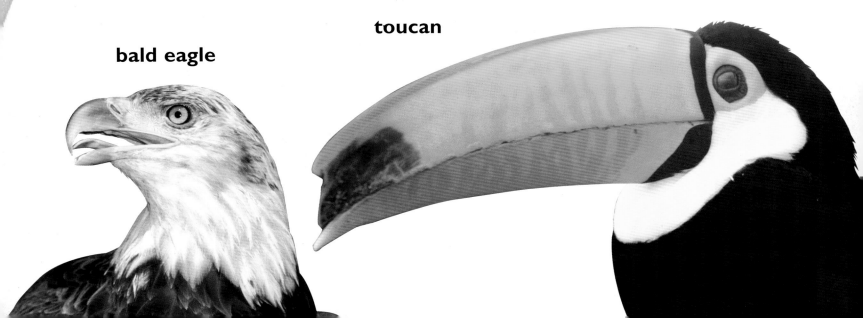

toucan

bald eagle

△ **Rockhopper penguins** have long yellow or orange feathers above their eyes. They often nest on clifftops, using pebbles or grass. They reach their colony by hopping from rock to rock, as their name suggests.

△ **After a winter at sea,** Snares Island penguins arrive at the islands of the same name, south of New Zealand. They return to these islands every August to breed again.

▽ **These Adélie penguins** are waddling about on an iceberg, off the coast of Antarctica. To climb out of the sea, penguins first dive down and then shoot out of the water at great speed, landing on their feet. To get back into the sea, they simply jump in.

◁ **Penguins** feed mainly on fish, squid and small shrimplike krill. They dive deep underwater, using their feet as rudders, and come to the surface regularly to breathe. Gentoo penguins can swim at up to 16 mph (27 kph).

Penguins

Like all the world's birds, penguins are covered with feathers. But penguin feathers are short and thick. They are waterproof, and keep the animals warm in cold seas.

Penguins have a horny beak for catching food. They also have a small pair of wings, but nevertheless, can't fly. They use their wings as flippers. These birds spend most of their time at sea and are fast, skilful swimmers.

There are 18 different kinds of penguin, and they all live near the coasts of the cold southern oceans. Many live in the frozen region of Antarctica.

emperor penguin

little blue penguin

▷ **The smallest penguins** are "little blues" standing 16 inches (40 cm) high. Emperor penguins are the biggest at 48 inches (120 cm) tall.

△ **Antarctic emperor penguins** keep their eggs and chicks on their feet, for warmth. It is the male bird who does this job, while the female feeds her young.

NEW WORDS
chick A baby bird, such as a young penguin.
krill Tiny shrimplike creatures that are eaten by penguins and whales.

A PENGUIN PLAYMATE
Pour sand into an empty plastic bottle and tape a washball to the top. Tape a cardboard beak to the head. Mix wallpaper paste and paste thin strips of newspaper over the penguin. When it's dry, paint the penguin white. Leave to dry again before painting the head, back and flippers black, leaving white circles for the eyes. You could use your penguin as a bookend.

Amphibians

Frogs, toads, newts, and salamanders belong to a group of animals called amphibians. They spend part of their lives on land and part in water, but amphibians don't live in the sea.

Amphibians go back to water when it is time to lay their eggs. Females may lay their eggs in or near a pond or stream. Most frogs and toads lay between 1,000 and 20,000 eggs. These large clusters of eggs are called spawn.

△ **Tree frogs** have round suckers at the end of their toes. These help them to grip trunks, branches, and even shiny leaves.

▷ **Large North American bullfrogs** can grow up to 8 inches (20 cm) long. This bullfrog has caught an earthworm, but they eat much larger prey too. A big bullfrog might catch a mouse or even a small snake.

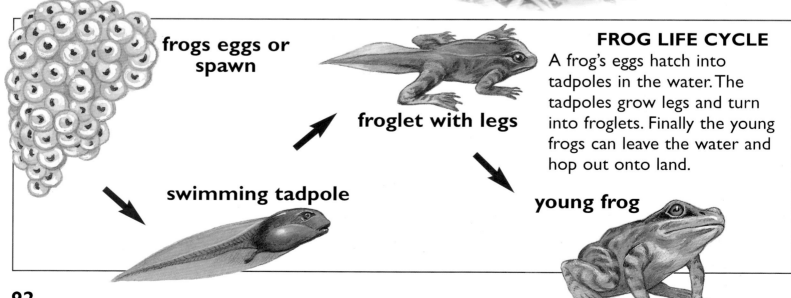

frogs eggs or spawn

froglet with legs

swimming tadpole

FROG LIFE CYCLE
A frog's eggs hatch into tadpoles in the water. The tadpoles grow legs and turn into froglets. Finally the young frogs can leave the water and hop out onto land.

young frog

△ **This smooth-skinned giant salamander** lives in the rivers, lakes, and cool, damp forests of western USA. It can grow to 12 inches (30 cm) long. Most salamanders are silent, but this one can make a low-pitched cry.

What are mouth-brooders?
A male mouth-brooding frog can gather up to 15 eggs with its tongue and put them in its mouth. But it doesn't eat the eggs. It keeps them in its vocal sac to turn into tadpoles. When the froglets are ready, they jump out.

▷ **Arrow-poison frogs** of South America are very poisonous. Females lay up to six eggs on land. When they hatch, the male carries the tadpoles on his back to a tree hole filled with water or to a water plant, so that they can begin life in water.

Toads usually have a rougher, bumpier skin than frogs which is often covered with warts. Toads usually live in drier places. They have wider bodies and shorter, less powerful legs, which means that they are not such good jumpers.

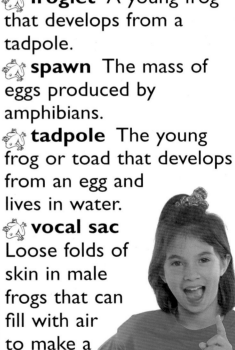

NEW WORDS

froglet A young frog that develops from a tadpole.

spawn The mass of eggs produced by amphibians.

tadpole The young frog or toad that develops from an egg and lives in water.

vocal sac Loose folds of skin in male frogs that can fill with air to make a noise.

△ **Frogs** have long back legs. These are good for swimming and we copy their action when we swim breaststroke. These powerful legs are also useful for jumping on land. Common frogs can leap about 2 feet (60 cm), and South African sharp-nosed frogs can jump over 10 feet (3 m)!

Female surinam toads keep their eggs in holes in their skin. The young toads develop in these holes.

Fish

There are more than 20,000 different kinds of fish in the world's oceans, lakes, and rivers. Like other animals, fish live in warm parts of the world, as well as in cold polar seas.

Many fish have streamlined bodies and fins, to help them swim. They have gills instead of lungs, so that they can breathe under water.

Fish have the same body temperature as the waters in which they live and swim.

◁ **The butterfly fish** has beautiful colors and strong contrasting markings.

▽ **The lionfish** has fins sticking out all over its body, and a row of poisonous spines. It grows up to 15 inches (38 cm) long.

△ **Some fish** have amazing defences. This porcupine fish has swollen up into a spiny ball. It must have sensed danger nearby.

▽ **Salmon** have to work very hard to make their way upriver from the ocean to breed. They swim against the current of the river and leap over the shallow, rocky parts.

NEW WORDS
breed To produce babies.
fin A thin flat part that sticks out of a fish's body and helps it to swim.
gill The parts of their bodies through which fishes breathe.
streamlined Shaped smoothly for moving faster.

▽ **The ray** has a flat body, which helps it glide along the bottom of the sea. Rays feed mainly on shellfish, which they crack open with their strong teeth. Some kinds of rays can sting with their tails.

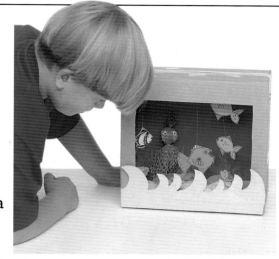

HOW FISH BREATHE

1. A fish takes in water through its mouth.

2. The water flows over its gills and oxygen passes into its bloodstream.

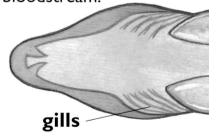

gills

3. The water is then pushed back out through the gill covers.

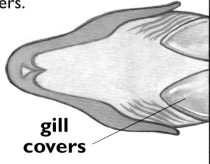

gill covers

▷ **Seahorses** look very strange. They swim in an upright position and live near seaweed, which they can hold on to with their tails. Seahorses are a fish which can change color.

▷ **This trumpet fish** is long and thin, growing up to 3 feet (0.9 m) long. Its eyes are set well back from its jaws. Compare its shape to the ray and the porcupine fish.

Electric eels kill fish and other sea animals with electric shocks from their tail. These big South American fish are up to 6 feet (1.8 m) long.

▽ **Moray eels** usually swim along with their mouths open, ready to catch smaller fish.

Insects

head

antennae

thorax

abdomen

△ **This wasp** shows the three basic body parts of an insect—a head, a thorax, and an abdomen. Its legs and wings are attached to the thorax, and its antennae to the head.

▽ **This honey bee** is collecting nectar and pollen from a flower. The bee will take the food to its nest, where it will be stored as honey.

Insects are tiny animals that are found all over the world—from scorching deserts to steaming rain forests and icy lakes.

Insects have no backbone, and they are protected by a hard, outer skeleton or shell. Because they are so small, they can fit into tiny places and don't need much food to live on. They all have six legs, and most have wings and can fly. Many insects have two pairs of wings, but flies have just one pair.

termite mound

food stores

queen's chamber

tunnel

egg chambers

▷ **Termites** live in colonies and build huge mounds as nests. Each colony is ruled by a king and a queen. Soldier termites defend the nest, and most of the termites are workers.

◁ **Ladybugs** are a kind of beetle. They feed on much smaller insects, called aphids and scale insects, which they find on plants. The ladybug's hard, outer wings protect the flying wings underneath.

▷ **Female mosquitoes** are bloodsuckers. They insert a needle-like tube into birds and mammals, including humans, and suck up a tiny amount of blood.

△ **Beetles** live just about everywhere on Earth. Some live in water, and many can fly. This horned beetle is found in Borneo, in Southeast Asia.

A single bee would have to visit more than 4,000 flowers to make one tablespoon of honey. A large beehive may contain 60,000 worker bees.

ZIGZAG LADYBUG
Fold a large piece of paper backward and forward into a zigzag. Then draw a ladybug shape at one end, making sure that a part of the ladybug's body joins each edge. Cut out the ladybug, but don't cut the zigzag edges. Unfold the paper and color in all your ladybugs. You could make a chain of buzzing bees too.

NEW WORDS
abdomen The lower or back part of an insect's body.
antennae An insect's very sensitive feelers, attached to its head.
aphid A tiny insect that feeds on plants.
termite Also called a white ant, this insect lives in a colony.
thorax The upper or front part of an insect's body, to which its wings and legs are attached.

◁ **Scorpions** have a poisonous sting in their tails, which they use to paralyse prey. They also have powerful claws.

▷ **A hunting spider** from Costa Rica in, Central America. But spiders also live in cold parts of the world.

△ **Trapdoor spiders** have a very clever system for catching insects. The spider digs a burrow, lines it with silk and covers the entrance with a trapdoor. Then it lies in wait. When an insect passes nearby, the spider feels the ground move. Then it jumps out and catches the insect, quickly dragging it into its burrow.

△ **Web-making spiders** feel the silk threads of the web move when an insect is caught. They tie their prey up in a band of silk.

◁ **Garden spiders** spin beautiful circular webs. These are easily damaged, and the spiders spend a lot of time repairing them. The webs show up well when the air outside is damp.

Spiders

Spiders are similar in some ways to insects, but they belong to a different group of animals called arachnids. Scorpions, ticks, and mites are arachnids too.

Spiders have eight legs, while insects have six. Many spiders spin silky webs to catch flies and other small insects. They have fangs for seizing their prey. Most spiders paralyze their prey with poison before they kill and eat them. But only a few spiders are poisonous to humans.

> **NEW WORDS**
> 🕷 **arachnid** A group of animals that includes spiders, scorpions, ticks, and mites.
> 🕷 **paralyze** To make something unable to move.
> 🕷 **spiderling** A young spider.

△ **Most spiders** and other arachnids have eight eyes. But spiders still do not see very well. They rely on touching things to know what is going on around them.

△ **There are about 40,000** different kinds of spider, and there can be many millions of each type. In a grassy meadow, there may be as many as 50 spiders in a square foot.

△ **A spider with its prey.** If spiders were not good hunters, the world would be overrun with insects.

◁ **Female spiders** lay up to 2,000 eggs, which they wrap in a bundle of silk threads. Spiderlings hatch from the eggs.

Mollusks and Crustaceans

Can squids shoot ink?
Squids and octopuses can shoot out a stream of inky fluid when they want to get away from enemies. The ink clouds the water and confuses the enemy, giving the mollusk time to escape.

Some mollusks, such as octopuses, have soft bodies. Others, such as snails, are protected by shells. Some mollusks live on land but many live in the sea.

Crustaceans get their name from their crusty covering. Most of them, such as crabs, lobsters, and shrimp, live in the sea. A few crustaceans, such as woodlice, live on land.

Mollusks and crustaceans all begin life as eggs, and most of them have a larva stage.

△ **Squids** are related to octopuses. They take in water and push it out again through a funnel behind their head. This acts like a jet engine and shoots them along backward.

△ **Hermit crabs** use the shells of sea snails for protection. Some kill and eat the snail to get both a meal and a home. When it outgrows the shell, the crab looks for a new one.

The world's largest crustacean is the giant spider crab, which has a legspan of almost 13 feet (4 m).

△ **Sallylightfoot crabs** live on the rocky shores of the Galapagos Islands, off South America. As they grow, they shed their shells and grow bigger ones. These measure up to 6 inches (15 cm) across.

◁ **Octopuses** are eight-armed molluscs. Many are very small, but the largest have tentacles up to 12 feet (3.5 m) long. Octopuses can change color according to their surroundings, so they can easily hide.

△ **Lobsters** are among the largest crustaceans. They walk across the seabed on four pairs of legs.

▷ Crabs' legs are made in such a way that they can walk sideways. The front pair of legs have strong pincers which they use for picking up food. They use the back pair of legs as paddles when they swim. Most crabs live in or near the sea.

△ **A garden snail's soft body** has a muscular foot, which it uses to creep along. The snail's whole body can be pulled safely into its shell if it is threatened by another animal.

NEW WORDS

legspan The widest distance between the legs at full stretch.

shed To let something fall off.

tentacle A long bendy body part, like an arm, that is used for feeling, moving and grasping.

TREASURE CHEST

Collect some empty shells on vacation and wash them out. Paint a box and stick some shells on the lid with glue. Paint the gaps with glue and sprinkle on some sand. Glue shells around the sides of the box in patterns. When the shells are firmly stuck, brush more glue on top to varnish them. Now you can lock away all your secrets—as well as any spare shells—in your treasure chest.

Early Life

This is blue-green algae, one of the simplest forms of life, seen through a microscope. It is made up of a skin surrounding a watery "soup," and has no complicated parts.

Life on Earth has been developing and changing over billions of years. Scientists now believe that the simplest forms of life began in the world's oceans, probably over three billion years ago.

We can only guess what the very first plants and animals looked like. But we think that many early sea animals had soft bodies, without shells, bones, or other hard parts. They included jellyfish, different kinds of worms, and other creatures related to starfishes.

◁ **These jellyfish,** sea pens, and worms lived in the world's oceans about 650 million years ago. They were mainly on the seabed.

NEW WORDS

algae Plants that grow in the sea, without true stems, leaves, or roots.

jellyfish A sea animal with an umbrella-shaped body like jelly.

sea pen A feather-shaped sea animal related to jellyfish.

starfish A sea animal that has the shape of a five-pointed star.

△ **The shallow coastal areas** of the early oceans were full of green, brown, and red algae, which we call seaweeds. Today, there are about 7,000 different kinds of seaweed. Most are found in warm, tropical waters.

How old are sharks?
The ancestors of today's sharks were swimming in the seas about 400 million years ago. They are one of the oldest animal groups with backbones still alive today.

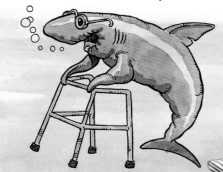

△ **Fast-moving, armor-plated fish** like this Coccosteus ruled the seas about 370 million years ago. A typical Coccosteus was about 16 inches (40 cm) long, and had sharp bony ridges and tusks inside its strong jaws. It could easily catch and eat slower-moving shellfish.

The first fishes had a head, a backbone and a tail, but no fins or jaws. They could not swim fast and sucked food into their mouths instead of biting it.

▽ **Scientists** thought that Coelacanths died out about 70 million years ago. But in 1938, a fisherman caught one in the Indian Ocean. These ancient fish grow up to 6 feet (2 m) long.

The Age of Amphibians

About 360 million years ago, some sea creatures left the water and crawled out onto land. Already there were many different fish in the sea, as well as plants and insects on land.

By now some animals could live on land and in water. We call these animals amphibians, which means "having a double life." Steamy swamps and forests were an ideal place for them to live. Amphibians laid their eggs in water. The eggs hatched into swimming tadpoles, and when they became adults, they moved onto the land. This is exactly how amphibians such as frogs and toads live today.

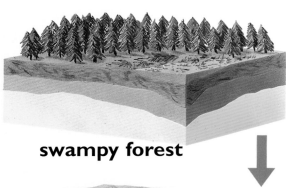

swampy forest

peat bog

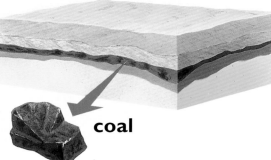

coal

△ **Dead leaves** and branches formed layers of plant material in the swampy forests of the early amphibians. This made peat, and when this was covered by rocks, the pressure turned it into coal.

▷ **Ichthyostega** was one of the first amphibians. It was about 3 feet (1 m) long. Giant dragonflies and many other insects lived among the tall, treelike ferns.

◁ **Ancient coal** has provided us with knowledge about the past, as well as fuel. Some leaves survived intact as the coal was formed and made fossils like this one.

▷ **This North American bullfrog** is a good example of a modern amphibian. Bullfrogs spend most of their time near water. All frogs breathe through lungs, as well as through their skin. Today there are about 4,000 different kinds of amphibians round the world, including frogs, toads, newts, and salamanders.

Early amphibians were much bigger than they are today. The early giants died out about 200 million years ago. But there is one exception, a giant salamander, which lives in China and can grow to a length of 6 feet (1.8 m).

PREHISTORIC LANDSCAPE
Use a large cereal box as a base, with the lid as a background. Cut and tape the box, line it with blue paper, cut out a volcano and stick it on. Use tissue paper for giant ferns, and put cellophane over some blue paper for a lake. Color some sand green with food coloring and sprinkle it on the base. Build rocks with stones and cones, and add a plastic dinosaur.

NEW WORDS
amphibian An animal that lives on land but lays its eggs in water.
dragonfly An insect with a long body and two pairs of thin wings.
peat Rotted plant material in the ground.
swamp An area of wet, low and marshy ground.

LIZARD HIPS AND BIRD HIPS

Scientists have divided dinosaurs into two main groups, according to the shapes of their hips. One group, including Tyrannosaurus (above right), had hips shaped like those of a modern lizard. The other group, which included Stegosaurus (below), had hips like a bird.

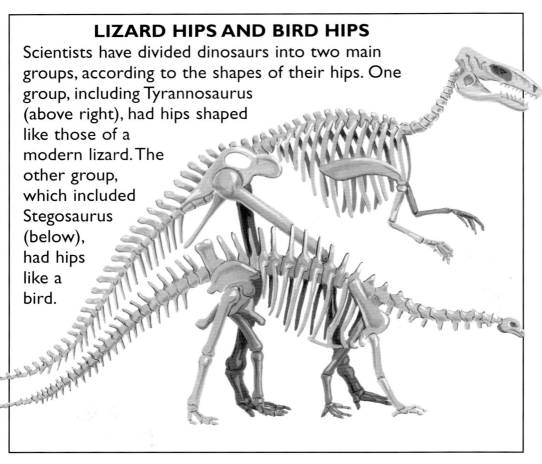

NEW WORDS

🦕 **badlands** Land where rocks have been worn away by wind and rain.

🦕 **sauropod** A general name for a gigantic lizard-hipped plant-eating dinosaur.

🦕 **habitat** The natural place on Earth where an animal or plant lives.

All the meat-eating dinosaurs and big four-legged plant eaters were lizard-hipped. The later bird-hipped dinosaurs were all plant eaters.

◁ **This scientist** is working at Dinosaur National Monument, Utah. More than 5,000 dinosaur fossils have been found there. The most common remains have been those of Stegosaurus.

▷ **This barrel-bodied plant-eater** used to be called Brontosaurus. But then it was found to be the same as earlier fossils called Apatosaurus, so the first name was chosen for this creature.

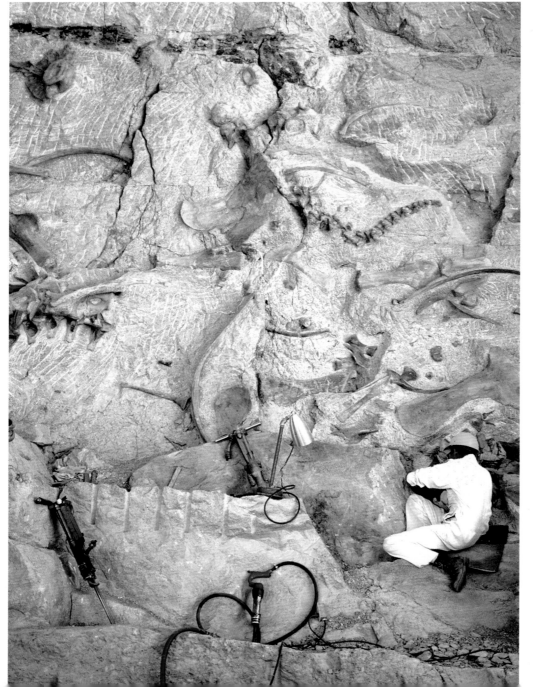

Dinosaurs

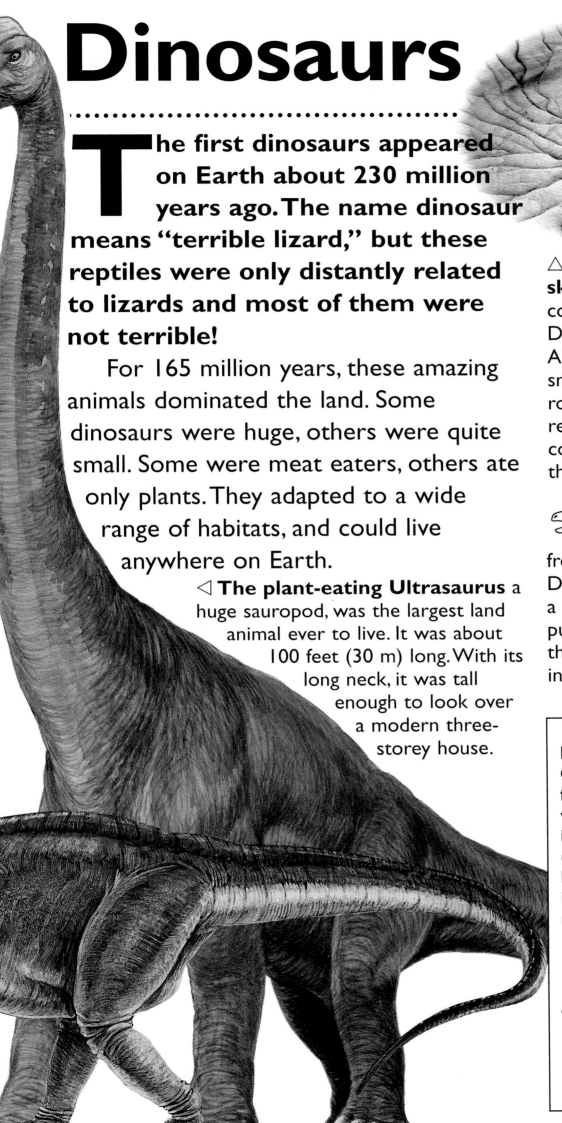

The first dinosaurs appeared on Earth about 230 million years ago. The name dinosaur means "terrible lizard," but these reptiles were only distantly related to lizards and most of them were not terrible!

For 165 million years, these amazing animals dominated the land. Some dinosaurs were huge, others were quite small. Some were meat eaters, others ate only plants. They adapted to a wide range of habitats, and could live anywhere on Earth.

◁ **The plant-eating Ultrasaurus** a huge sauropod, was the largest land animal ever to live. It was about 100 feet (30 m) long. With its long neck, it was tall enough to look over a modern three-storey house.

△ **Hundreds of dinosaur skeletons** have been collected in the badlands of Dinosaur Provincial Park, in Alberta, Canada. Rain and snow have worn away the rocks, uncovering the reptile remains. Dinosaur collectors first rushed to the area in the early 1900s.

Today's scientists move large bones from regions such as Dinosaur Provincial Park by a helicopter or truck. They put the pieces together, and the skeletons are displayed in a nearby museum.

SIZES
Dinosaurs came in all sizes. Compsognathus was a small, fast-moving, meat-eater with very sharp teeth. It was 28 inches (70 cm) to 56 inches (1.4 m) long, including its long tail. It probably ate large insects, lizards, and mouselike mammals.

Meat-eating Dinosaurs

The dinosaur carnivores, or meat eaters, were powerfully built animals. They walked upright on their two back legs, and their shorter arms ended in hands with clawed fingers.

The big meat eaters, such as Tyrannosaurus, had a huge head on a short neck. They had very strong, sharp teeth. Nearly all meat eaters had a long, muscular tail, which they carried straight out behind them. This helped them to balance their heavy weight. Their strong back legs made meat eaters the fastest of all the dinosaurs.

△ **Oviraptor** had a tall crest on the top of its head. This birdlike creature fed on other dinosaurs' eggs, which it scooped up in its three-fingered hands and cracked open with its strong jaws. Oviraptors were about 6 feet (2 m) long.

Which was fastest?
We don't know how fast dinosaurs could run, but scientists think Struthiomimus was one of the fastest. It was 13 feet (4 m) long, looked like an ostrich and may have reached speeds of 30 mph (50 km/h).

◁ **Allosaurus** was one of the biggest meat eaters before Tyrannosaurus. It was 36 feet (11 m) long. We don't know what color dinosaurs were, but some might have been brightly colored.

Ostrichlike Struthiomimus was an omnivore: it ate animals and plants. Its long claws could hook leaves and fruit from low trees. It also fed on insects and lizards.

MAKE A MEAT EATER'S TOOTH

Model a big ball of self-hardening clay into the shape of a meat-eating dinosaur's tooth. Texture the surface and mark it so that it looks ancient and fossilized. It may take up to two days for the tooth to harden. When it is hard, paint your ferocious tooth.

Baryonyx claw

Tyrannosaurus tooth

△ **Baryonyx** had long, curved thumb-claws. Tyrannosaurus had enormous teeth. They were up to 7 inches (18 cm) long, with sharp edges like steak knives. Tooth finds have helped to tell us what different dinosaurs fed on.

NEW WORDS

🦖 **Age of Dinosaurs** The long period of time when dinosaurs lived on Earth.

🦖 **fossilized** Changed into a fossil.

🦖 **muscular** Powerful, with well-developed muscles.

🦖 **omnivore** An animal that eats all kinds of food: both meat and plants.

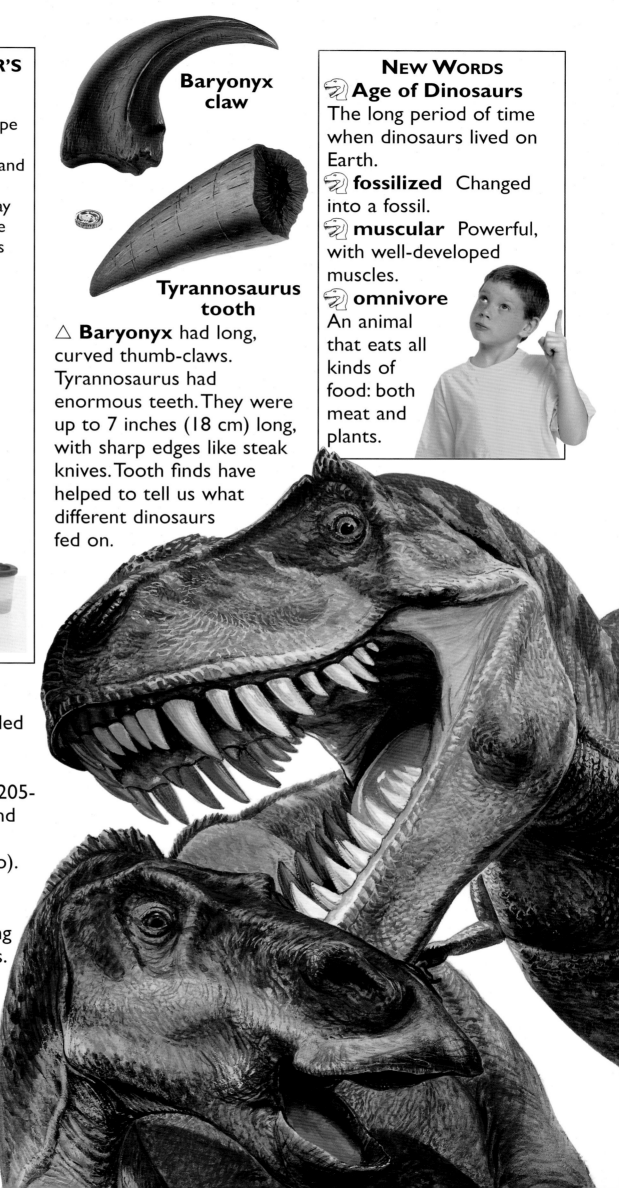

🦖 **The Age of the Dinosaurs** is divided into three periods: the Triassic (240-205 million years ago), the Jurassic (205-138 million years ago) and the Cretaceous period (138-65 million years ago).

▷ **Tyrannosaurus** was about 40 feet (12 m) long and weighed over 6 tons. Its forward-facing eyes helped it to judge distance well as it moved in to attack smaller dinosaurs. Its tiny arms look feeble but held sharp claws.

Plant-eating Dinosaurs

Which had the longest neck?
Mamenchisaurus, a huge plant eater found in China, had the longest neck of any animal ever known. Its neck was 50 feet (15 m) long—longer than eight tall men lying head to toe!

The dinosaur herbivores, or plant eaters, fed on the vegetation they could reach. Small herbivores ate roots and plants on the ground, and others may have reared up on their back legs to reach higher leaves.

The long-necked sauropods, such as Diplodocus, were tall enough to reach the treetops. These huge animals must have spent nearly all their time eating.

NEW WORDS

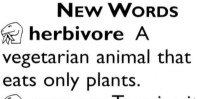 **herbivore** A vegetarian animal that eats only plants.

rear up To raise itself on its back legs.

stud A curved lump or knob.

vegetation Living plants, including twigs and the leaves of trees.

Scutellosaurus was a tiny plant eater, about the size of a modern cat. It had rows of bony studs along its back and tail, to protect it from attack by any larger meat eaters. It could walk or run on its back legs, as well as on all fours.

IGUANODON

This large, heavy dinosaur was a peaceful plant eater that could stand and walk either on its back legs or on all fours. It had spiked thumbs, which it may have used to defend itself if it was attacked by a hungry meat eater.

◁ **Long-necked plant eaters** may also have reared up to reach even higher treetops. Diplodocus picked leaves off with its front teeth, but had no back teeth for chewing.

The huge shoulder bones of Ultrasaurus were 9 feet (2.7 m) long, much longer than the tallest human. Its hip bones were also bigger than a man. Ultrasaurus was about 100 feet (30 m) long.

DIG UP A DIPLODOCUS

Cut up straws for bones and make them into a complete skeleton on a cardboard base. Brush each straw with glue and fix them firmly into position. Leave the straws to dry, and then brush more glue between the bones and around the whole skeleton. Sprinkle all over with sand. After a few minutes, tip the surplus sand onto newspaper. Then you'll have your very own fossilized Diplodocus!

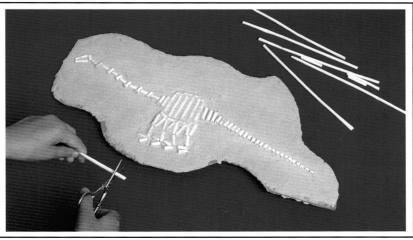

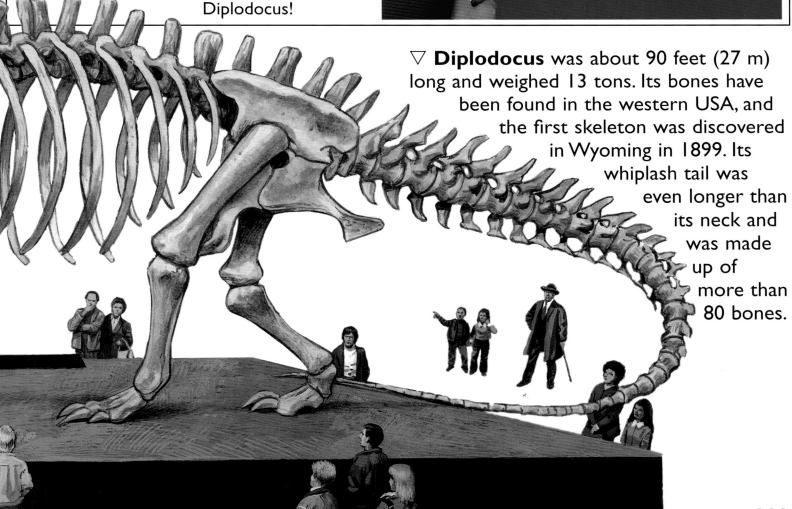

▽ **Diplodocus** was about 90 feet (27 m) long and weighed 13 tons. Its bones have been found in the western USA, and the first skeleton was discovered in Wyoming in 1899. Its whiplash tail was even longer than its neck and was made up of more than 80 bones.

Helmets, Spines, and Armor

Big, slow-moving animals need to protect themselves against fast, fierce meat eaters. Many plant-eating dinosaurs had some form of armor-plating to offer this protection.

Some dinosaurs had plates and spines running down their back and tail. Others had spikes that grew in their skin. They even had a bony club at the end of their tail, which was a powerful weapon against attackers. One group of dinosaurs had thick, bony skulls, which they used to head-butt each other during fights.

△ **The largest** bone-headed dinosaur, Pachycephalosaurus, had a thick, dome-shaped skull. This head-butting creature was 15 feet (4.6 m) long.

Styracosaurus lived on Earth about 75 million years ago, and fossils have been found in the USA and Canada.

Triceratops' teeth were hard on one side. The other, softer side wore down faster, leaving a sharp cutting edge.

Stegosaurus was about 30 feet (9 m) long, but it had a small head and its brain was little bigger than a walnut. Dinosaur skulls were filled mainly with muscle and bone.

△ **Styracosaurus** had long spikes sticking out of a bony frill. It also had a large nose horn, like a modern rhinoceros.

112

CARDBOARD STEGOSAURUS

Cut the sides off some large cardboard boxes and tape them together. Draw the long dinosaur body shape of a Stegosaurus (see the photograph, right) and cut it out. Make plates and tail spikes from cardboard, and use egg cups for scales. Paint the egg cups green and stick them on the body. Fasten the plates with tape. Crush up lots of pieces of tissue paper and glue them all over your dinosaur's body. You could use a bottle top for a beady, prehistoric eye!

◁ **Triceratops** means "three-horned face." Although the horns were for self-defence, scientists think that these dinosaurs may also have fought one another.

△ **Euoplocephalus** had slabs of bony armor, spikes on its back, and a clubbed tail. It used its powerful muscles to swing its tail at any enemies.

NEW WORDS

armor A protective covering for the body.

club Something heavy, like a tail, that can be used as a weapon.

frill A fold of skin and bone for protection around the neck.

head-butt To use its head to hit another dinosaur on the head.

▷ **This is Meteor Crater,** in Arizona. It is over a half a mile (1 km) across and was made about 50,000 years ago when a meteorite hit Earth. Some scientists think a much bigger asteroid might have struck Earth 65 million years ago.

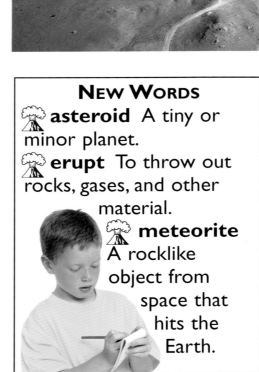

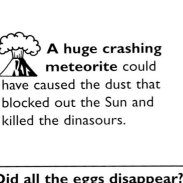 **A huge crashing meteorite** could have caused the dust that blocked out the Sun and killed the dinasours.

Did all the eggs disappear?
Another theory is that small mammals raided dinosaur nests and ate so many eggs all at once that there were no more dinosaur babies. This seems an unlikely story.

NEW WORDS
asteroid A tiny or minor planet.
erupt To throw out rocks, gases, and other material.
meteorite A rocklike object from space that hits the Earth.

▷ **If we had not found fossilized bones,** we would not even know that dinosaurs ever existed.

▽ **It could be that many vast volcanoes** erupted over a period of a few years or even longer. This might have made the Earth too hot, poisoned the air and blotted out the Sun.

Dinosaurs Die Out

Dinosaurs became extinct, or died out, about 65 million years ago. The great reptiles of the sea and air disappeared at the same time. We are not sure why this happened.

It could be that at that time the Earth became covered in dust and smoke, blocking out sunlight for months or even years. Plants and many animals, including dinosaurs, could not have survived this catastrophe.

▽ **Plant eaters** such as Saltasaurus (below) and meat eaters like Tyrannosaurus, were among the last known dinosaurs. The meat eaters ran out of food once the plant eaters had died out!

Early Man

Human like creatures that we call "southern apes" lived in Africa about four million years ago. We know that about two million years later, a kind of human that we call "handy man" was making and using stone tools.

Hundreds of thousands of years after that, "upright man" found out how to use fire. Next came Neanderthal man. He evolved about 250,000 years ago and died out about 30,000 years ago. He was the predecessor of "modern man," or Homo sapiens, which means "wise man." He evolved successfully, and developed farming, kept animals and made cave paintings. These were our human ancestors.

△ **We think that Homo erectus,** or "upright man," was the first to use fire. This was useful for cooking food, keeping warm and scaring animals away from shelters such as caves. Hot stones may also have been used to make simple ovens.

▽ **Prehistoric paintings** in caves at Lascaux, France, were found by four teenage boys in 1940. The paintings, of animals were made about 17,000 years ago.

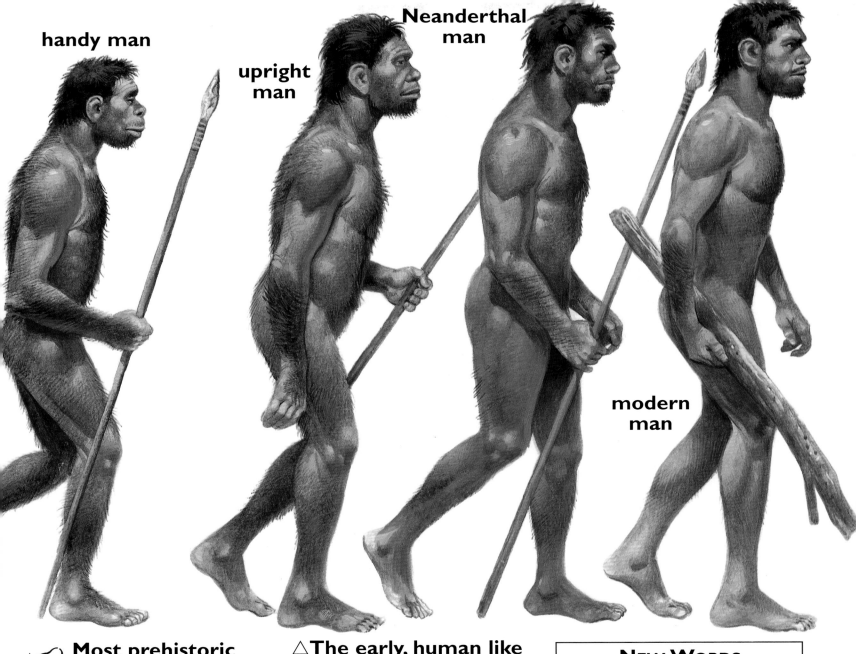

handy man

upright man

Neanderthal man

modern man

 Most prehistoric people were hunters and gatherers. They would hunt large animals such as mammoths and woolly rhinoceroses. They would gather fruits, berries, and seeds too.

△**The early, human like** "southern ape" was called Australopithecus. Next came "handy man" (Homo habilis), who could make stone tools, then "upright man," who used fire. We modern humans are from the group called "wise man" (Homo sapiens).

NEW WORDS

ancestor A person or an animal from which another one is descended.

prehistoric Relating to very ancient times before writing was invented.

STONE PAINTINGS

You can turn a collection of smooth pebbles or stones into a friendly snake. Give your stones a good wash and then let them dry thoroughly before you start painting. Use the biggest stone for the head, and then go down in size all the way to the tip of the tail. Paint the body of your snake with green poster paint, and let this dry before adding yellow markings, a pair of eyes and a forked tongue. When the stones are dry, arrange them into a slithering snake shape.

MAKE A MUMMY

Take a doll and an old sheet. Tear the sheet into strips and wrap the doll from head to toe in these bandages. Make a coffin from a shoebox. The Egyptians put green stone scarab beetles along with their mummies, and you could paint one on the end of the coffin. When you want your doll back, just take the bandages off your Egyptian mummy!

⚠ When a body was mummified, the dead person's internal organs (liver, lungs, stomach and intestines) were removed and stored in special jars.

⚠ Cats were sacred to the ancient Egyptians and were also mummified when they died.

▷ **It probably took 100,000 men** more than 20 years to build the Great Pyramid. They used more than two million heavy blocks of stone. The pharaoh's burial chamber was deep inside the pyramid.

▽ **The wall paintings** found in ancient tombs have told us a lot about the way ancient Egyptians lived.

▷ **Pharaohs** were sometimes buried inside huge stone pyramids. The Great Pyramid is still standing at Giza, near Cairo, the modern capital of Egypt.

Ancient Egypt

Thousands of years ago, people hunted around the River Nile. Then they settled there and began to farm the land.

Ancient Egypt was ruled by kings, called pharaohs. The Egyptians believed the spirit of their hawk god, Horus, entered a new pharaoh and made him a god too. They also believed in life after death, and pharaohs were buried with things they wanted to take on to the next world.

△ **Egyptian noblemen** hunted in the marshes around the Nile. They used throwing sticks to bring down birds.

NEW WORDS
⚒ **mummy** A dead body specially treated so that it does not decay.
⚒ **pharaoh** A king of ancient Egypt.
⚒ **tomb** A place where someone is buried.

▷ **King Tutankhamun** died at only 18 years old. He was buried in a tomb in the Valley of the Kings, near the ancient city of Thebes. This gold mask was found among the treasure in Tutankhamun's tomb.

◁ **The stone monument** of the Great Sphinx has a man's head and a lion's body. It stands 66 feet (20 m) high, near the pyramids at Giza. The Sphinx was carved 4,500 years ago.

Ancient Greece

Hermes   Aphrodite   Zeus   Hera   Demeter   Hades

◁ **Zeus** was king of the Greek gods, and Hera was his wife. Hermes was the gods' messenger, Aphrodite was the goddess of love, Demeter goddess of grain, and Hades god of the dead.

About 2,800 years ago, a new civilisation began in Greece. The ancient Greeks produced many fine buildings and cities. They wrote plays, studied music, and began a system of government which allowed people a say in how their state was run.

Athens became the biggest and richest city state in ancient Greece, with a very well-trained army and a powerful navy. Sparta controlled the southern part of Greece. All true Spartans had to be warriors, and boys were trained to fight from the age of seven.

NEW WORDS

city state A state made up of a city and the surrounding areas.
column A pillar used to hold up a building.
government The ruling and running of a state or country.
state An organized community, such as a country.
trireme A warship with three banks of oars on each side.

◁ **The Parthenon** was the main temple of the goddess Athene. Today, its ruins stand on a rocky hill in Athens called the Acropolis.

▷ **The Greeks** were the first to build permanent stone theaters. In ancient times the actors were all men, and they wore masks to show the sort of character they were playing.

Corinthian

Ionic

Doric

◁ **The ancient Greeks** developed special ways to decorate the tops of the columns, or pillars, that they used to support their beautiful buildings. Doric was the earliest order, or type. Then came Ionic, and finally Corinthian.

When and where were the first Olympic Games?
The first Olympic Games were held in 776 BC in Olympia, a place dedicated to the god Zeus. The first athletes carried shields and wore helmets, but no clothes!

DRAMATIC MASKS
Put a big plate on cardboard and draw around it. Then cut out the circle. Hold the cutout in front of your face and ask a friend to mark the position of your eyes. Put the cutout down and cut out two eye holes to see through. Paint a happy or a sad face, and tape on a popsicle handle. Finally, stick on card ears and ribbon hair.

Rich Greek boys had their own slave. It was his job to look after the boy, take him to school and help with his homework.

▷ **The most famous** types of Greek warship were biremes and triremes. A bireme had two banks of rowers on each side, and a trireme had three banks. Soldiers fought on the flat deck of the ships, which could go very fast and be used to ram others.

Ancient Rome

The great city of Rome began as a small village on one of seven hills, about 2,700 years ago. As the city grew in size and power, the Romans conquered other peoples in Italy.

Then the Roman armies created an empire that stretched around the Mediterranean Sea and reached as far as France and England. Roman soldiers built thousands of miles of good, straight roads throughout their empire. Some Roman roads still exist to this day.

▷ **The Roman Empire** began under Augustus, who became the first emperor in 27BC. This great leader set the style for later emperors.

According to legend, Rome was founded by two twins, Romulus and Remus. Abandoned as babies, the brothers were fed milk by a female wolf and later found by a shepherd.

Roman cities always had fresh water. It was brought from the hills to street fountains and houses along aqueducts.

△ **In AD79,** Mount Vesuvius suddenly erupted and covered the nearby Italian town of Pompeii with volcanic ash. The town was buried and thousands of people were killed.

What was the Roman circus?
In ancient Rome, the circus was an oval-shaped arena where chariot races were held. These were very popular sporting events, and up to 250,000 people could pack into the biggest circus in Rome.

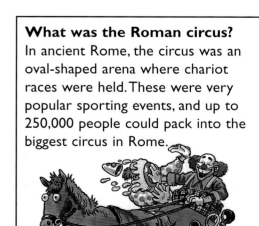

▷ **Julius Caesar** was a great Roman general in the last years before the first emperor. He was stabbed to death in 44 BC.

▽ **The Forum** in ancient Rome was an open public square. Citizens went there to discuss any important questions of the day together.

▽ **The Colosseum** was the largest amphitheater of ancient Rome. It could hold about 50,000 spectators.

▷ **Centurions** were officers in the Rom army. Each one commanded about a hundred soldiers, who made up a century. The army was very well trained and extremely powerful.

The Middle Ages

△ **Printing** had not yet been invented. Books were copied by hand by monks. They were often beautifully decorated in bright colors.

▽ **Kings and nobles** built castles to protect themselves against enemies. Inside they were often cold and damp, but there was always a large kitchen. Meals were eaten in the Great Hall.

The Middle Ages is the name that is usually given to roughly a thousand years of history, starting in about AD500. This medieval period covers the history between ancient and modern times in Europe.

During the Middle Ages, European countries were ruled by a king or an emperor, who generally owned all the land. The land was divided among the ruler's most important men, who were called nobles. The nobles were supported by knights, who were trained in battle. Peasants lived and worked on the nobles' and knights' land, growing food for both themselves and for their lord.

△ **In medieval towns** there were no proper drains, and people threw their trash in the street. Jugglers, actors, and others put on entertainments, and there were shops selling all sorts of different goods.

▷ **Stained-glass windows** were used to decorate medieval churches. They often told stories from the Bible, using small pieces of colored glass held together by lead.

▽ **Knights** took part in tournaments, where they fought against each other on horseback. One knight tried to knock another to the ground by hitting him with his lance.

NEW WORDS
⬥ **knight** A man who was brought up to serve as a soldier.
⬥ **lance** A long spear.
⬥ **medieval** To do with the Middle Ages.
⬥ **noble** A person high up the social scale.
⬥ **peasant** A farmer or worker on the land.
⬥ **stained** Colored glass used in windows.

Index